Native American Rights

Other Books in the Issues on Trial Series:

Native American Rights

Uma Kukathas, Book Editor

GREENHAVEN PRESS
A part of Gale, Cengage Learning

GALE
CENGAGE Learning

Detroit • New York • San Francisco • New Haven, Conn • Waterville, Maine • London

Christine Nasso, *Publisher*
Elizabeth Des Chenes, *Managing Editor*

© 2008 Greenhaven Press, a part of Gale, Cengage Learning

For more information, contact:
Greenhaven Press
27500 Drake Rd.
Farmington Hills, MI 48331-3535
Or you can visit our Internet site at gale.cengage.com.

For product information and technology assistance, contact us at

Gale Customer Support, 1-800-877-4253
For permission to use material from this text or product, submit all requests online at www.cengage.com/permissions

Further permissions questions can be emailed to permissionrequest@cengage.com

Articles in Greenhaven Press anthologies are often edited for length to meet page requirements. In addition, original titles of these works are changed to clearly present the main thesis and to explicitly indicate the author's opinion. Every effort is made to ensure that Greenhaven Press accurately reflects the original intent of the authors. Every effort has been made to trace the owners of copyrighted material.

Cover photograph reproduced by permission of AP Images.

LIBRARY OF CONGRESS CATALOGING-IN-PUBLICATION DATA

Native American rights / Uma Kukathas, book editor.
    p. cm. -- (Issues on trial)
    Includes bibliographical references and index.
    ISBN-13: 978-0-7377-4076-9 (hardcover)
    1. Indians of North America--Legal status, laws, etc. 2. Indians of North America--Civil rights. 3. Indians of North America--Legal status, laws, etc.--Cases. 4. Indians of North America--Civil rights--Cases. I. Kukathas, Uma.
    KF8205.N3855 2008
    342.7308'72--dc22

                                     2008010057

Printed in the United States of America
2 3 4 5 6 7 12 11 10 09 08

Contents

Chapter 1: Affirming the Limits of Tribal Sovereignty

Chapter 2: Upholding Congressional Power over Tribes

Chapter 3: Compensating Indians for Illegal Seizure of Tribal Lands

Foreword

The U.S. courts have long served as a battleground for the most highly charged and contentious issues of the time. Divisive matters are often brought into the legal system by activists who feel strongly for their cause and demand an official resolution. Indeed, subjects that give rise to intense emotions or involve closely held religious or moral beliefs lay at the heart of the most polemical court rulings in history. One such case was *Brown v. Board of Education* (1954), which ended racial segregation in schools. Prior to *Brown*, the courts had held that blacks could be forced to use separate facilities as long as these facilities were equal to that of whites.

For years many groups had opposed segregation based on religious, moral, and legal grounds. Educators produced heartfelt testimony that segregated schooling greatly disadvantaged black children. They noted that in comparison to whites, blacks received a substandard education in deplorable conditions. Religious leaders such as Martin Luther King Jr. preached that the harsh treatment of blacks was immoral and unjust. Many involved in civil rights law, such as Thurgood Marshall, called for equal protection of all people under the law, as their study of the Constitution had indicated that segregation was illegal and un-American. Whatever their motivation for ending the practice, and despite the threats they received from segregationists, these ardent activists remained unwavering in their cause.

Those fighting against the integration of schools were mainly white southerners who did not believe that whites and blacks should intermingle. Blacks were subordinate to whites, they maintained, and society had to resist any attempt to break down strict color lines. Some white southerners charged that segregated schooling was *not* hindering blacks' education. For example, Virginia attorney general J. Lindsay Almond asserted, "With the help and the sympathy and the love and respect of the white people of the South, the colored man has risen under that educational process to a place of eminence and respect throughout the nation. It has served him well." So when the Supreme Court ruled against the segregationists in *Brown*, the South responded with vociferous cries of protest. Even government leaders criticized the decision. The governor of Arkansas, Orval Faubus, stated that he would not "be a party to any attempt to force acceptance of change to which the people are so overwhelmingly opposed." Indeed, resistance to integration was so great that when black students arrived at the formerly all-white Central High School in Arkansas, federal troops had to be dispatched to quell a threatening mob of protesters.

Nevertheless, the *Brown* decision was enforced, and the South integrated its schools. In this instance, the Court, while not settling the issue to everyone's satisfaction, functioned as an instrument of progress by forcing a major social change. Historian David Halberstam observes that the *Brown* ruling "deprived segregationist practices of their moral legitimacy. . . . It was therefore perhaps the single most important moment of the decade, the moment that separated the old order from the new and helped create the tumultuous era just arriving." Considered one of the most important victories for civil rights, *Brown* paved the way for challenges to racial segregation in many areas, including on public buses and in restaurants.

In examining *Brown*, it becomes apparent that the courts play an influential role—and face an arduous challenge—in shaping the debate over emotionally charged social issues. Judges must balance competing interests, keeping in mind the high stakes and intense emotions on both sides. As exemplified by *Brown*, judicial decisions often upset the status quo and initiate significant changes in society. Greenhaven Press's Issues on Trial series captures the controversy surrounding influential court rulings and explores the social ramifications of such decisions from varying perspectives. Each anthology highlights one social issue—such as the death penalty, students' rights, or wartime civil liberties. Each volume then focuses on key historical and contemporary court cases that helped mold the issue as we know it today. The books include a compendium of primary sources—court rulings, dissents, and immediate reactions to the rulings—as well as secondary sources from experts in the field, people involved in the cases, legal analysts, and other commentators opining on the implications and legacy of the chosen cases. An annotated table of contents, an in-depth introduction, and prefaces that overview each case all provide context as readers delve into the topic at hand. To help students fully probe the subject, each volume contains book and periodical bibliographies, a comprehensive index, and a list of organizations to contact. With these features, the Issues on Trial series offers a well-rounded perspective on the courts' role in framing society's thorniest, most impassioned debates.

Introduction

When Europeans first arrived in what is now the United States more than five hundred years ago, the lives of the indigenous peoples changed radically. The several hundred tribes who were the original inhabitants of the American land were suddenly subjected to diseases to which they had no immunity. Chicken pox and measles wiped out huge numbers (some estimate it at 80 percent of the population). Conflicts with the new invaders took the lives of many others, as Europeans began to lay claim to the lands the Indians had occupied for centuries.

In the eighteenth century, before the United States declared itself a nation, several colonies signed treaties with Indian nations. As early as 1722, a peace treaty was signed between the Assateague and Pocomoke Indians in the colony of Maryland. While the colonists were at war with Britain, they enlisted the support of Native American tribes and made treaties with them. In 1778 a treaty was signed at Fort Pitt that recognized the Delaware as a sovereign nation and guaranteed its territorial rights in return for guarantees of the tribe's support of the Revolutionary government in the war. Other treaties similarly acknowledged other Indian tribes as independent nations, in return for their recognition of the United States.

In the next ninety years, the federal government made more than 370 treaties with Indian nations, two-thirds of them being land cessions. Indians ceded some 450 million acres in return for less than $90 million. It is now acknowledged by historians that nearly all of these treaties were forced on the Native American nations. Also, few of the treaties were honored by the federal government (some treaties, but far fewer, were broken by the tribes). Among numerous injustices, land that Indians had been promised was taken from them and given to white settlers, and native communities were forced to leave their traditional homelands.

For Native Americans, the history of their rights in the United States has thus been one of broken promises, of forced removal from their lands, and of an ensuing erosion of their traditional way of life and ability to practice their culture and traditions. Much of Native American history has been the struggle of Indians to maintain their sovereignty and rights to their land after the conquest and settlement by Europeans. In addition to being forcibly removed from land that they regard as having been stolen from them, they have suffered the indignity of being subjected to laws they believe to be in direct conflict with their understanding of the natural world, their values, and their religious practices.

In the early nineteenth century, when Indian tribes recognized that their rights were being infringed upon by unfair practices by the state and federal governments and by individual settlers, they turned to the courts for help. However, early court cases reveal that, despite constitutional provisions outlining Indian sovereignty, they were in practical terms not entitled to those protections or the same rights under the law as whites. For example, in 1828, the state of Georgia passed a series of laws stripping Cherokee Indians of their rights. The laws also authorized Cherokee removal from lands sought after by the state. The Cherokee protested that according to treaties that had been negotiated with them as an independent nation, they were guaranteed both their land and independence. They sought fresh negotiations with president Andrew Jackson and Congress. When those failed, they turned to the Supreme Court and sought an injunction against Georgia to prevent its carrying out these laws.

The Court ruled in that landmark case that the Cherokee were not a sovereign nation but a "domestic dependent nation" subject to the United States, as a ward is subject to its guardian. Thus the Supreme Court could not interfere with the state of Georgia and its laws that would have the effect of stripping the Cherokee of their rights. The tragic result of this case was the forced removal in 1838 of the Cherokee from their land. In one of the saddest episodes of United States history, Indian men, women, and children were herded by army forces into makeshift forts with minimal facilities and food and forced to march a thousand miles. Thousands died along the way on what is now referred to as the "Trail of Tears."

Since that early episode, Native Americans have repeatedly experienced the erosion of their basic human rights—including rights to property, freedom of religion, and free speech. Federal policies regarding Indians over the next hundred years, say Native American leaders, included extermination, termination, forced removal and relocation, the outlawing of traditional religions, and the destruction of sacred places. Native American activists have pointed out that in the nineteenth and twentieth centuries, the government condemned the traditions, beliefs, and customs of native peoples and endeavored to assimilate them by such policies as the redistribution of land under the General Allotment Act of 1887 and the forcible removal of Indian children from their families to boarding schools. These crimes were perpetrated by the United States government using legal means and with public and congressional support, leaving Indians with few means to fight for what was theirs.

In 1924, Congress granted citizenship to all Native Americans born in the United States, and Indians thus gained some rights because of that status. However, many states still prohibited Indians from voting. A study called the Meriam Report that was published in 1928 brought to public attention the status of Native Americans living in the United States. It described the effects of oppressive federal policies that had destroyed native cultures and societies. It showed how early policies had resulted in ongoing poverty, exploitation, and discrimination. The Meriam Report spurred the passage of the

1934 Indian Reorganization Act, which returned some land to Native Americans and urged tribes to engage in active self-government.

After the Civil Rights movement of the 1960s, Native Americans pressed for more of the rights they had been denied by the U.S. government. Indian leaders took state and federal governments to court to protect what was left of tribal lands or to recover property that had been taken illegally. They challenged treaty violations and in 1967 won the first of many victories guaranteeing land and water rights. The following year, the American Indian Movement (AIM) was founded to establish international recognition of Indian treaty rights and to help assist individual Indians.

While Native Americans have made considerable strides in fighting for the rights denied them since European colonization, the legal battles they continue to fight show that there is more to be done in terms of gaining their full complement of rights as American citizens and to redress the damage done by centuries of ill treatment. For example, the Lakota Sioux continue to fight for the return of the Black Hills, refusing the $105 million settlement they were offered in monetary compensation, insisting that their sacred land cannot be bought. Native Americans also continue to go to the courts to fight for their freedom of religion, arguing for access to religious sites, freedom to use peyote and eagle feathers in religious ceremonies, and the right to hunt whales. Some have also called for the United States government to publicly acknowledge its denial of Indian rights for centuries, as was done by the Australian prime minister in February 2008 when he apologized to Aborigines for past wrongs. A resolution has been introduced in the U.S. Senate to extend a formal apology from the United States to tribal governments and native people nationwide, but it has not yet been passed.

Affirming the Limits of Tribal Sovereignty

Case Overview

Cherokee Nation v. Georgia (1831)

In 1828, gold was discovered in the Cherokee territory of Georgia. To facilitate white settlers' access to land and to force the Cherokee to move, in December 1828, the state of Georgia enacted a series of laws that stripped the Cherokee Nation of their rights. Tribal Chief John Ross led a delegation to Washington to try to resolve the matter. He found congressional support, but president Andrew Jackson supported Georgia's desire to extend her laws over the Cherokee. In May 1830, Congress endorsed Jackson's policy and passed the Indian Removal Act, authorizing the president to exchange Indian land for land west of the Mississippi.

Ross and the Cherokee Nation decided to take legal action. They hired a white lawyer, William Wirt, to defend them. Ross went straight to the Supreme Court and asked for an injunction forbidding Georgia to remove the Cherokee. Wirt argued that Georgia's laws were intended to "annihilate the Cherokees as a political society," and, further, that the Cherokee Nation was a "foreign nation" in the sense of the U.S. Constitution and law . . . and thus not subject to Georgia's jurisdiction. The Supreme Court, said Wirt, should render null and void all Georgia laws pertaining to Cherokee lands because they violated the U.S. Constitution as well as treaties between the United States and the Cherokee. The Court refused to act unless Wirt showed that the Cherokee were in fact a foreign nation.

In the ensuing case, Georgia, an ardent supporter of states' rights, did not send any legal representation. Wirt argued that the Cherokee had incontestable rights to the lands they occupied in Georgia based on several treaties. Further, he argued, they constituted an independent nation and had been so regarded by the United States in its many treaties with them.

The justices hearing the case—John Marshall, John MacLean, Henry Baldwin, William Johnson, Joseph Story, and Smith Thompson—deliberated for several days but could not come to a unanimous decision. Two-thirds of the court eventually ruled against the Cherokees' request for an injunction. Speaking for the majority of the court, chief justice John Marshall handed down his decision on March 18, 1831. He rejected Wirt's argument that the Cherokee were a sovereign nation, holding they were "domestic dependent nations" subject to the United States as a ward is to its guardian. American Indian territory, he said, was part of the United States but not subject to action by individual states. Associate justice Smith Thompson later wrote a dissenting opinion to the public upholding the claims of the Cherokee Nation. He argued that even though the Cherokee had been under the protection of the United States, this in no way diminished their sovereignty as stipulated under treaties.

By 1838 the Cherokee were stripped of all their lands. That year, over seven thousand soldiers forced the Cherokee to leave what was left of their territory to relocate to Oklahoma. As they were forced to move thousands of miles to the west, more than four thousand Cherokee perished. This westward journey came to be known as the "Trail of Tears."

> "[The Indians] are in a state of pupilage. Their relation to the United States resembles that of a ward to his guardian."

The Court's Decision: The Cherokee Nation Is Not a Foreign Nation

John Marshall

John Marshall, a leader of the Federalist Party, was the fourth chief justice of the United States, serving from 1801 until his death in 1835. The longest-serving chief justice in Supreme Court history, Marshall was prominent in the development of the American legal system and helped shape the judiciary into an independent and influential branch of government. The following is Marshall's deciding opinion in Cherokee Nation v. Georgia, *one of the first cases in which Native Americans pressed their legal rights to the U.S. Supreme Court. The Cherokee requested an injunction to prevent the state of Georgia from driving them off their land and enacting laws that would annihilate their political existence. The tribe argued that they formed an autonomous foreign state over which neither individual states nor the federal government could claim dominion. Marshall, writing for the Court, acknowledged that the Cherokee and other Native American tribes were "gradually sinking" beneath the "superior policy" of the United States. However, he insisted that the Court could not base its decision on sympathy for the tribe's plight. First, Marshall declared, the Court had to determine whether it had jurisdiction to hear the case at all. The Cherokee*

John Marshall, majority opinion, *The Cherokee Nation v. The State of Georgia*, U.S. Supreme Court, 1831.

had argued they were a foreign state, saying the tribe was a distinct political society that managed its own affairs, and that both colonial and U.S. governments had regarded them as a state by negotiating treaties with them. However, Marshall concluded that they were not a foreign state since it was located within the geographical and jurisdictional boundaries of the United States and because the tribe had acknowledged they were under "protection" by the federal government. Thus, he argues, "their relation to the United States resembles that of a ward to his guardian." Therefore, according to Marshall, the Cherokee and other Native American tribes should be classified not as sovereign but as "domestic dependent nations."

This bill is brought by the Cherokee nation, praying an injunction to restrain the state of Georgia from the execution of certain laws of that state, which, as is alleged, go directly to annihilate the Cherokees as a political society, and to seize, for the use of Georgia, the lands of the nation which have been assured to them by the United States in solemn treaties repeatedly made and still in force.

If courts were permitted to indulge their sympathies, a case better calculated to excite them can scarcely be imagined. A people once numerous, powerful, and truly independent, found by our ancestors in the quiet and uncontrolled possession of an ample domain, gradually sinking beneath our superior policy, our arts and our arms, have yielded their lands by successive treaties, each of which contains a solemn guarantee of the residue, until they retain no more of their formerly extensive territory than is deemed necessary to their comfortable subsistence. To preserve this remnant, the present application is made.

Before we can look into the merits of the case, a preliminary inquiry presents itself. Has this court jurisdiction of the cause?

Does the Court Have Jurisdiction?

The third article of the constitution describes the extent of the judicial power. The second section closes an enumeration of the cases to which it is extended, with 'controversies' 'between a state or the citizens thereof, and foreign states, citizens, or subjects.' A subsequent clause of the same section gives the supreme court original jurisdiction in all 16 cases in which a state shall be a party. The party defendant may then unquestionably be sued in this court. May the plaintiff sue in it? Is the Cherokee nation a foreign state in the sense in which that term is used in the constitution?

The counsel for the plaintiffs have maintained the affirmative of this proposition with great earnestness and ability. So much of the argument as was intended to prove the character of the Cherokees as a state, as a distinct political society, separated from others, capable of managing its own affairs and governing itself, has, in the opinion of a majority of the judges, been completely successful. They have been uniformly treated as a state from the settlement of our country. The numerous treaties made with them by the United States recognize them as a people capable of maintaining the relations of peace and war, of being responsible in their political character for any violation of their engagements, or for any aggression committed on the citizens of the United States by any individual of their community. Laws have been enacted in the spirit of these treaties. The acts of our government plainly recognize the Cherokee nation as a state, and the courts are bound by those acts.

Are the Cherokee a Foreign State?

A question of much more difficulty remains. Do the Cherokees constitute a foreign state in the sense of the constitution?

The counsel have shown conclusively that they are not a state of the union, and have insisted that individually they are aliens, not owing allegiance to the United States. An aggregate of aliens composing a state must, they say, be a foreign state. Each individual being foreign, the whole must be foreign.

This argument is imposing, but we must examine it more closely before we yield to it. The condition of the Indians in relation to the United States is perhaps unlike that of any other two people in existence. In the general, nations not owing a common allegiance are foreign to each other. The term foreign nation is, with strict propriety, applicable by either to the other. But the relation of the Indians to the United States is marked by peculiar and cardinal distinctions which exist no where else.

The Indian territory is admitted to compose a part of the United States. In all our maps, geographical treatises, histories, and laws, it is so considered. In all our intercourse with foreign nations, in our commercial regulations, in any attempt at intercourse between Indians and foreign nations, they are considered as within the jurisdictional limits of the United States, subject to many of those restraints which are imposed upon our own citizens. They acknowledge themselves in their treaties to be under the protection of the United States; they admit that the United States shall have the sole and exclusive right of regulating the trade with them, and managing all their affairs as they think proper; and the Cherokees in particular were allowed by the treaty of Hopewell, which preceded the constitution, 'to send a deputy of their choice, whenever they think fit, to congress.' Treaties were made with some tribes by the state of New York, under a then unsettled construction of the confederation, by which they ceded all their lands to that state, taking back a limited grant to themselves, in which they admit their dependence.

Indians Are Wards of the Government

Though the Indians are acknowledged to have an unquestionable, and, heretofore, unquestioned right to the lands they occupy, until that right shall be extinguished by a voluntary cession to our government; yet it may well be doubted whether those tribes which reside within the acknowledged boundaries of the United States can, with strict accuracy, be denominated foreign nations. They may, more correctly, perhaps, be denominated domestic dependent nations. They occupy a territory to which we assert a title independent of their will, which must take effect in point of possession when their right of possession ceases. Meanwhile they are in a state of pupilage. Their relation to the United States resembles that of a ward to his guardian.

They look to our government for protection; rely upon its kindness and its power; appeal to it for relief to their wants; and address the president as their great father. They and their country are considered by foreign nations, as well as by ourselves, as being so completely under the sovereignty and dominion of the United States, that any attempt to acquire their lands, or to form a political connexion with them, would be considered by all as an invasion of our territory, and an act of hostility.

These considerations go far to support the opinion, that the framers of our constitution had not the Indian tribes in view, when they opened the courts of the union to controversies between a state or the citizens thereof, and foreign states.

In considering this subject, the habits and usages of the Indians, in their intercourse with their white neighbours, ought not to be entirely disregarded. At the time the constitution was framed, the idea of appealing to an American court of justice for an assertion of right or a redress of wrong, had perhaps never entered the mind of an Indian or of his tribe. Their appeal was to the tomahawk, or to the government. This was well understood by the statesmen who framed the constitution of the United States, and might furnish some reason for omitting to enumerate them among the parties who might sue in the courts of the union. Be this as it may, the peculiar relations between the United States and the Indians occupying our territory are such, that we should feel much difficulty in considering them as designated by the term foreign state, were there no other part of the constitution which might shed light on the meaning of these words. But we think that in construing them, considerable aid is furnished by that clause in the eighth section of the third article; which empowers congress to 'regulate commerce with foreign nations, and among the several states, and with the Indian tribes.'

In this clause they are as clearly contradistinguished by a name appropriate to themselves, from foreign nations, as from the several states composing the union. They are designated by a distinct appellation; and as this appellation can be applied to neither of the others, neither can the appellation distinguishing either of the others be in fair construction applied to them. The objects, to which the power of regulating commerce might be directed, are divided into three distinct classes—foreign nations, the several states, and Indian tribes. When forming this article, the convention considered them as entirely distinct. We cannot assume that the distinction was lost in framing a subsequent article, unless there be something in its language to authorize the assumption.

Tribes Are Not Foreign Nations

The counsel for the plaintiffs contend that the words 'Indian tribes' were introduced into the article, empowering congress to regulate commerce, for the purpose of removing those doubts in which the management of Indian affairs was involved by the language of the ninth article of the confederation. Intending to give the whole power of managing those affairs to the government about to be instituted, the convention conferred it explicitly; and omitted those qualifications which embarrassed the exercise of it as granted in the confederation. This may be admitted without weakening the construction which has been intimated. Had the Indian tribes been foreign nations, in the view of the convention, this exclusive power of regulating intercourse with them might have been, and most probably would have been, specifically given, in language indicating that idea, not in language contradistinguishing them from foreign nations. Congress might have been empowered 'to regulate commerce with foreign nations, including the Indian tribes, and among the several states.' This language would have suggested itself to statesmen who considered the Indian tribes as foreign nations, and were yet desirous of mentioning them particularly.

It has been also said, that the same words have not necessarily the same meaning attached to them when found in different parts of the same instrument: their meaning is controlled by the context. This is undoubtedly true. In common language the same word has various meanings, and the peculiar sense in which it is used in any sentence is to be determined by the context. This may not be equally true with respect to proper names. Foreign nations is a general term, the application of which to Indian tribes, when used in the American constitution, is at best extremely questionable. In one article in which a power is given to be exercised in regard to foreign nations generally, and to the Indian tribes particularly, they are mentioned as separate in terms clearly contradistinguishing them from each other. We perceive plainly that the constitution in this article does not comprehend Indian tribes in the general term 'foreign nations;' not we presume because a tribe may not be a nation, but because it is not foreign to the United States. When, afterwards, the term 'foreign state' is introduced, we cannot impute to the convention the intention to desert its former meaning, and to comprehend Indian tribes within it, unless the context force that construction on us. We find nothing in the context, and nothing in the subject of the article, which leads to it.

The court has bestowed its best attention on this question, and, after mature deliberation, the majority is of opinion that an Indian tribe or nation within the United States is not a foreign state in the sense of the constitution, and cannot maintain an action in the courts of the United States.

A serious additional objection exists to the jurisdiction of the court. Is the matter of the bill the proper subject for judicial inquiry and decision? It seeks to restrain a state from the forcible exercise of legislative power over a neighbouring people, asserting their independence; their right to which the state denies. On several of the matters alleged in the bill, for example on the laws making it criminal to exercise the usual powers of self government in their own country by the Cherokee nation, this court cannot interpose; at least in the form in which those matters are presented.

That part of the bill which respects the land occupied by the Indians, and prays the aid of the court to protect their possession, may be more doubtful. The mere question of right might perhaps be decided by this court in a proper case with proper parties. But the court is asked to do more than decide on the title. The bill requires us to control the legislature of Georgia, and to restrain the exertion of its physical force. The propriety of such an interposition by the court may be well questioned. It savours too much of the exercise of political power to be within the proper province of the judicial department. But the opinion on the point respecting parties makes it unnecessary to decide this question.

If it be true that the Cherokee nation have rights, this is not the tribunal in which those rights are to be asserted. If it be true that wrongs have been inflicted, and that still greater are to be apprehended, this is not the tribunal which can redress the past or prevent the future.

The motion for an injunction is denied.

> "[The Cherokee] have never been, by conquest, reduced to the situation of subjects to any conqueror, and thereby lost their separate national existence."

Dissenting Opinion: The Cherokee Nation Is a Weak but Sovereign Nation

Smith Thompson

Smith Thompson, appointed to the Supreme Court by Andrew Jackson, served as associate justice from 1823 until his death in 1843. A staunch opponent of chief justice John Marshall, Thompson, in his dissenting opinion in Cherokee Nation v. Georgia, *firmly upholds the claims of the Cherokee that Marshall denied in his decision. Thompson's opinion was not delivered to the Court but written later at the request of the chief justice and published by the Court's reporter. In the case, the Cherokee had requested an injunction to prevent the state of Georgia from driving them off their land. The Marshall Court decided that it did not have jurisdiction to hear the case, because the Cherokee were not a foreign sovereign state, as they claimed. In his dissent, Thompson claims that the Cherokee have always been dealt with by the United States as sovereign people who had exercised exclusive dominion over their territory, even though they from time to time yielded up portions of their land by treaty. Thompson points out that the Native Americans' "progress . . . in civilization" did nothing to destroy their national or foreign character, since they had been permitted to maintain a separate and*

Smith Thompson, dissenting opinion, *The Cherokee Nation v. The State of Georgia*, U.S. Supreme Court, 1831.

distinct government. Thus in his dissent Thompson offers a different understanding of "protection" than had Marshall, arguing that a political entity can have protection and still be a nation. Just because a weaker state signs a protection treaty does not mean it loses its sovereignty, declares Thompson, so long as it retains self-government, and by these standards the Cherokee are a sovereign nation.

Entertaining different views of the questions now before us in this case, and having arrived at a conclusion different from that of a majority of the Court, and considering the importance of the case and the constitutional principle involved in it, I shall proceed, with all due respect for the opinion of others, to assign the reasons upon which my own has been formed.

In the opinion pronounced by the Court, the merits of the controversy between the State of Georgia and the Cherokee Indians have not been taken into consideration. The denial of the application for an injunction has been placed solely on the ground of want of jurisdiction in this Court to grant the relief prayed for. It became, therefore, unnecessary to inquire into the merits of the case. But thinking as I do that the Court has jurisdiction of the case, and may grant relief, at least in part, it may become necessary for me, in the course of my opinion, to glance at the merits of the controversy, which I shall, however, do very briefly, as it is important so far as relates to the present application.

Before entering upon the examination of the particular points which have been made and argued, and for the purpose of guarding against any erroneous conclusions, it is proper that I should state that I do not claim for this Court the exercise of jurisdiction upon any matter properly falling under the denomination of political power. Relief to the full extent prayed by the bill may be beyond the reach of this Court. Much of the matter therein contained by way of complaint would seem to depend for relief upon the exercise of political power, and, as such, appropriately devolving upon the executive, and not the judicial department of the government. This Court can grant relief so far only as the rights of person or property are drawn in question, and have been infringed.

Relief for Past Injury

It would very ill become the judicial station which I hold to indulge in any remarks upon the hardship of the case, or the great injustice that would seem to have been done to the complainants according to the Statement in the bill, and which, for the purpose of the present motion I must assume to be true. If they are entitled to other than judicial relief, it cannot be admitted that, in a Government like ours, redress is not to be had in some of its departments, and the responsibility for its denial must rest upon those who have the power to grant it. But believing as I do that relief to some extent falls properly under judicial cognizance, I shall proceed to the examination of the case under the following heads.

1. Is the Cherokee Nation of Indians a competent party to suc in this Court?

2. Is a sufficient case made out in the bill to warrant this Court in granting any relief?

3. Is an injunction the fit and appropriate relief?

By the Constitution of the United States it is declared, that the judicial power shall extend to all cases in law and equity, arising under this Constitution, the laws of the United States, and treaties made or which shall be made under their authority, &c. to controversies between two or more States, &c. and between a State or the citizens thereof and foreign states, citizens or subjects.

Are the Cherokee a Foreign State?

The controversy in the present case is alleged to be between a foreign state and one of the States of the union, and does not, therefore, come within the Eleventh Amendment of the Constitution, which declares that the judicial power of the United States shall not be construed to extend to any suit in law or equity commenced or prosecuted against one of the United States by citizens of another State, or by citizens or subjects of any foreign state. This amendment does not, therefore, extend to suits prosecuted against one of the United States by a foreign state. The Constitution further provides that, in all cases where a State shall be a party, the Supreme Court shall have original jurisdiction. Under these provisions in the Constitution, the complainants have filed their bill in this Court, in the character of a foreign state, against the State of Georgia; praying an injunction to restrain that State from committing various alleged violations of the property of the Nation, claimed under the laws of the United States, and treaties made with the Cherokee Nation.

That a State of this union may be sued by a foreign state when a proper case exists and is presented is too plainly and expressly declared in the Constitution to admit of doubt; and the first inquiry is whether the Cherokee Nation is a foreign state within the sense and meaning of the Constitution.

The terms "state" and "nation" are used in the law of nations, as well as in common parlance, as importing the same thing, and imply a body of men, united together to procure their mutual safety and advantage by means of their union. Such a society has its affairs and interests to manage; it deliberates, and takes resolutions in common, and thus becomes a moral person, having an understanding and a will peculiar to itself, and is susceptible of obligations and laws. Nations being composed of men naturally free and independent, and who, before the establishment of civil societies, live together in the state of nature, nations or sovereign states, are to be considered as so many free persons, living together in a state of nature. Every nation that governs itself, under what form soever, without any dependence on a foreign power is a sovereign state. Its rights are naturally the same as those of any other state. Such are moral persons who live together in a natural society under the law of nations. It is sufficient if it be really sovereign and independent—that is, it must govern itself by its own authority and laws. We ought, therefore, to reckon in the number of sovereigns those states that have bound themselves to another more powerful, although by an unequal alliance. The conditions of these unequal alliances may be infinitely varied; but whatever they are, provided the inferior ally reserves to itself the sovereignty or the right to govern its own body, it ought to be considered an independent state. Consequently, a weak state, that, in order to provide for its safety, places itself under the protection of a more powerful one without stripping itself of the right of government and sovereignty, does not cease on this account to be placed among the sovereigns who acknowledge no other power. Tributary and feudatory states do not thereby cease to be sovereign and independent states, so long as self-government and sovereign and independent authority is left in the administration of the state.

Testing the character and condition of the Cherokee Indians by these rules, it is not perceived how it is possible to escape the conclusion that they form a sovereign state. They have always been dealt with as such by the Government of the United States, both before and since the adoption of the present Constitution. They have been admitted and treated as a people governed solely and exclusively by their own laws, usages, and customs within their own territory, claiming and exercising exclusive dominion over the same, yielding up by treaty, from time to time, portions of their land, but still claiming absolute sovereignty and self-government over what remained unsold. And this has been the light in which they have, until recently, been considered from the earliest settlement of the country by the white people. And indeed, I do not understand it is denied by a majority of the Court that the Cherokee Indians form a sovereign state according to the doctrine of the law of nations, but that, although a sovereign state, they are not considered a foreign state within the meaning of the Constitution.

Why the Tribe Is a Foreign State

Whether the Cherokee Indians are to be considered a foreign state or not is a point on which we cannot expect to discover much light from the law of nations. We must derive this knowledge chiefly from the practice of our own government and the light in which the Nation has been viewed and treated by it.

That numerous tribes of Indians, and among others the Cherokee Nation, occupied many parts of this country long before the discovery by Europeans is abundantly established by history, and it is not denied but that the Cherokee Nation occupied the territory now claimed by them long before that period. It does not fall within the scope and object of the present inquiry to go into a critical examination of the nature and extent of the rights growing out of such occupancy, or the justice and humanity with which the Indians have been treated, or their rights respected.

That they are entitled to such occupancy so long as they choose quietly and peaceably to remain upon the land cannot be questioned. The circumstance of their original occupancy is here referred to merely for the purpose of showing that, if these Indian communities were then, as they certainly were, nations, they must have been foreign nations to all the world, not having any connexion, or alliance of any description with any other power on earth. And if the Cherokees were then a foreign nation, when or how have they lost that character, and ceased to be a distinct people, and become incorporated with any other community?

They have never been, by conquest, reduced to the situation of subjects to any conqueror, and thereby lost their separate national existence, and the rights of self-government, and become subject to the laws of the conqueror. Whenever wars have taken place, they have been followed by regular treaties of peace, containing stipulations on each side according to existing circumstances; the Indian Nation always preserving its distinct and separate national character. And notwithstanding we do not recognize the right of the Indians to transfer the absolute title of their lands to any other than ourselves, the right of occupancy is still admitted to remain in them, accompanied with the right of self-government according to their own usages and customs, and with the competency to act in a national capacity although placed under the protection of the whites, and owing a qualified subjection so far as is requisite for public safety. But the principle is universally admitted that this occupancy belongs to them as matter of right, and not by mere indulgence. They cannot be disturbed in the enjoyment of it, or deprived of it without their free consent, or unless a just and necessary war should sanction their dispossession.

Progress Does Not Change Tribe's Status

In this view of their situation, there is as full and complete recognition of their sovereignty, as if they were the absolute owners of the soil. The progress made in civilization by the Cherokee Indians cannot surely be considered as in any measure destroying their national or foreign character so long as they are permitted to maintain a separate and distinct government; it is their political condition that constitutes their foreign character, and in that sense must the term "foreign" be understood as used in the Constitution. It can have no relation to local, geographical, or territorial position. It cannot mean a country beyond [the] sea. Mexico or Canada is certainly to be considered a foreign country in reference to the United States. It is the political relation in which one government or country stands to another which constitutes it foreign to the other. The Cherokee territory being within the chartered limits of Georgia does not affect the question. When

Georgia is spoken of as a State, reference is had to its political character, and not the boundary, and it is not perceived that any absurdity or inconsistency grows out of the circumstance that the jurisdiction and territory of the State of Georgia surround or extend on every side of the Cherokee territory. It may be inconvenient to the State, and very desirable that the Cherokees should be removed, but it does not at all affect the political relation between Georgia and those Indians. Suppose the Cherokee territory had been occupied by Spaniards or any other civilized people, instead of Indians, and they had from time to time ceded to the United States portions of their lands precisely in the same manner as the Indians have done, and in like manner retained and occupied the part now held by the Cherokees, and having a regular government established there; would it not only be considered a separate and distinct nation or state, but a foreign nation, with reference to the State of Georgia or the United States. If we look to lexicographers, as well as approved writers, for the use of the term "foreign," it may be applied with the strictest propriety to the Cherokee Nation.

I have endeavoured to show that the Cherokee Nation is a foreign state, and, as such, a competent party to maintain an original suit in this Court against one of the United States. The injuries complained of are violations committed and threatened upon the property of the complainants, secured to them by the laws and treaties of the United States. Under the Constitution, the judicial power of the United States extends expressly to all cases in law and equity arising under the laws of the United States and treaties made or which shall be made under the authority of the same. . . .

Upon the whole, I am of opinion,

1. That the Cherokees compose a foreign state within the sense and meaning of the Constitution, and constitute a competent party to maintain a suit against the State of Georgia.

2. That the bill presents a case for judicial consideration arising under the laws of the United States and treaties made under their authority with the Cherokee Nation, and which laws and treaties have been, and are threatened to be still further, violated by the laws of the State of Georgia referred to in this opinion.

3. That an injunction is a fit and proper writ to be issued to prevent the further execution of such laws, and ought therefore to be awarded.

And I am authorised by my brother [justice Joseph] Story to say that he concurs with me in this opinion.

"[The Marshall Trilogy of] opinions are the house in which American Indian advocates . . . rise each morning—and it is a house filled with an iron cold of the deepest hour."

The Court's Decision in *Cherokee Nation* Is Racist

Matthew L.M. Fletcher

Matthew L.M. Fletcher is an assistant professor at Michigan State University College of Law and director of the Indigenous Law and Policy Center. In the following viewpoint, Fletcher comments on both the Court's decision and the dissenting opinion in Cherokee Nation v. Georgia, *whose ruling denied the Cherokees' status as a foreign sovereign nation and declared it legal for the state of Georgia to enact laws removing them from their land. Fletcher begins by asserting that chief justice John Marshall's opinion in* Cherokee *and two other related cases fundamental to current Indian law, known as the "Marshall Trilogy," are the "iron cold" house in which Native American leaders and policy makers are forced to live to this day. The author goes on to show that the fragmented opinions by the justices in* Cherokee *point to the contentiousness of the issue and the fractures within the judiciary itself.* Cherokee *and the other cases in the Marshall Trilogy, Fletcher explains, are important today because of the notions of "protection" that are presented in those opinions. Fletcher also says it should be noted too as significant for current Indian law that Marshall's opinion in* Cherokee *was deeply rac-*

Matthew L.M. Fletcher, "The Iron Cold of the Marshall Trilogy," *North Dakota Law Review*, vol. 82, 2006. Copyright © 2006 North Dakota Law Review. Reproduced by permission.

ist. His view that an Indian tribe could not be a state because Indian people were too "low" has repercussions to the present day, Fletcher maintains, and its racist foundations require that the house of Indian law be updated and retrofitted to reflect today's knowledge.

> *This house is old. For two hundred years a woman has risen in the iron cold of the deepest hour.*

> *—Louise Erdrich*

Students of American Indian law cannot—and should not— escape from reading the three famous opinions of Chief Justice John Marshall that expounded for the first time in the halls of the United States Supreme Court the bases for federal Indian common law—the opinions we now refer to as the "Marshall Trilogy." These foundational principles resonate today, more than eighteen decades after the Court put them into words. . . . These three decisions, *Johnson v. M'Intosh*, *Cherokee Nation v. Georgia*, and *Worcester v. Georgia*, written in the obtuse legalese of the day, identified the contours of American Indian law as they remain today in the modern era. These opinions are the house in which American Indian advocates, leaders, and policymakers rise each morning—and it is a house filled with an iron cold of the deepest hour. . . .

A Fragmented Decision

The holding in *Cherokee Nation v. Georgia* is simple—Indian tribes are not "foreign State[s]" as envisioned in Article III, section 2, paragraph 1 of the Constitution. Chief Justice Marshall, writing for only one other Justice, wrote the lead opinion. Justices [William] Johnson and [Henry] Baldwin concurred in the outcome, writing opinions weighed against Indian interests. At the Chief Justice's informal request Justice [Smith] Thompson wrote a dissent in which Justice [Joseph] Story concurred. It was unusual for the Marshall Court to render such a fragmented decision, evidence that the Marshall

39

Court had begun to split apart as the Chief Justice aged and that the question of state authority in Indian Country was a contentious one.

In the lead opinion, Chief Justice Marshall began by holding that Indian tribes were "states" (but not States of the Union) as envisioned by the Constitution, a question contested by the Justices concurring in the result. . . .

The Chief Justice then answered in the negative the question whether this Indian tribe could be considered a "foreign State". . .

The derogation by the State of Georgia of the Cherokee Nation—a community with written laws and a functioning government, a sitting delegation in Congress, a treaty relationship with the United States, and a surplus of food—would continue. . . .

Protection or Dependence?

The important overlay of this debate involves the boilerplate treaty language of "protection." The various Justices debated the meaning of "protection" as being either an invitation to dependence or a recognition of political distinctiveness.

Justice Baldwin's *Cherokee Nation* concurrence was the first to focus on the word "protection" in the Northwest Ordinance and the Treaty of Hopewell. The Treaty of Hopewell explained the purpose of the treaty and, by extension, the meaning of "protection": "For the benefit and comfort of the Indians, and for the prevention of injuries and aggressions on the part of the citizens or Indians. . . ." Despite this explicit language that tends to lead one (perhaps) in the other direction, Justice Baldwin took the meaning of this language to be that Indian tribes had a "dependent character;" that "protection" was "indenture of servitude;" and that the Cherokee Nation, as a result of the treaty, was "dependent on and appendant to the state government." He concluded that the "protection" language and the context of the Treaty of

Hopewell granted Congress the right to decide the "internal" affairs should it wish to at a later date, a precursor to the plenary power Congress would later take up in force.

According to Chief Justice Marshall in the *Johnson* case, Indian tribes included characteristics of both "dependent" or "distinct" nations, a sort of middle ground. But in *Cherokee Nation*, writing for "the Court" (but really only for himself and one other Justice), he famously labeled Indian tribes "domestic dependent nations" as a new legal term of art created from whole cloth in order to avoid classifying Indian tribes as either states or foreign nations. In this case, the Chief Justice denigrates Indian tribes a great deal: "[T]hey are in a state of pupilage. Their relation to the United States resembles that of a ward to his guardian." In this opinion, Indian tribes appear to be dependent in large extent to the United States. Justice Johnson, in his *Cherokee Nation* concurring opinion, avoided the guardian-ward dichotomy and used the term "master and conqueror" in reference to the United States. In Justice Johnson's view, Indian tribes existed in a state of "feudal dependence" to the United States—in other words, complete and utter dependence on the order of slaves or serfs.

Justice Thompson's dissent (joined by Justice Story) in *Cherokee Nation* suggested a different reading of the word "protection." Drawing on the venerable [Swiss philosopher and diplomat Emmerich de] Vattel, Justice Thompson found that weaker states signing treaties of protection do not, as a side-effect, lose their sovereignty. All that is required for a weaker state to retain statehood is a reservation of the right to self-government, a staple in American Indian treaties. "Protection" and nationhood are not mutually exclusive. Presaging modern Indian affairs where all Indian tribes (save one) are located within the boundaries of a state, Justice Thompson argued that "[t]he Cherokee territory being within the chartered limits of Georgia, does not affect the question." Moreover, state courts had defined "protection" to be consistent with the retention of sovereignty. Justice Thompson would have found that the Cherokee Nation was a "foreign nation" in the meaning of the Constitution. Justice Thompson's version of "protection" did not mean all-encompassing dependency, but instead, significant political independence. . . .

Racism Informed Decisions

No discussion of the Trilogy is complete without a full reckoning of the racism inherent in the holdings or the racism of the reasoning behind the holdings. Indians are labeled "fierce savages," prone to massacring helpless non-Indians, and always, always, always "gradually sinking." Justice Baldwin took the view that the earliest Indian cases before the Court gave the members an opportunity to nip Indian claims in the bud before they became a problem, as in the "maxim *obsta principiis*" ["resist from the start"].

The superiority of Euro-American culture was never in question. As Euro-American populations advanced, "that of the Indians necessarily receded." The entire Marshall Court, it appears, was bamboozled by one of the greatest lies ever perpetrated about Indian people—that Indians were hunters and were not (and could not) be farmers. Contemporaneous to the Marshall Trilogy, Henry Schoolcraft, the well-connected Jacksonian charged with surveying the Old Northwest, wrote in 1827 that "[o]ld green fields appeared in spots [on Mackinac Island], which have been formerly cultivated by Indians." A Detroit newspaper editorial gaped in 1831, "The largest corn I ever saw was raised on these prairies." And the Cherokee Nation had a surplus of food. According to the Court, however, Euro-American farmers advanced, pushing the Indian "hunters" away into the "unbroken forest." Under their reasoning, Indian lands used for hunting were not owned; in fact, they were "vacant."

Justice Johnson's opinion in *Cherokee Nation* may be one of the most racist opinions ever published by a Supreme Court

Justice. Justice Johnson's opinion was that an Indian tribe could not be a "state," as defined in international law, for the reason that Indian people were too "low" for that designation. Justice Johnson's opinion is littered with the proposition that Indians were no more than "hunters." He seems to focus on this term because of a throwaway line in the Treaty of Hopewell, a treaty signed by the Cherokee Nation and the fledgling United States after the Revolutionary War, defining the territorial lands of the Nation by a rhetorical term as "hunting grounds." The twisted irony of Justice Johnson's opinion is that he accepts that the Cherokee Nation is moving away from being a mere "race of hunters" to a viable and "approved form[] of civil government." As such, he reasoned, because the Nation was moving away from its "hunter" state to a more civilized state, it made perfect sense for state law to apply. Justice Johnson found the federal goal of civilizing Indians laudable, but believed that, due to the "restless, warlike, and signally cruel" nature of Indian people and the "inveterate habits and deep seated enmity" of Indian tribes, such a goal had failed. Such language gives great fodder for commentators to decry federal Indian law as racist. . . .

Advocates Cannot Rely on Racist Rulings

There's a lot of great language in the Trilogy that supports tribal advocates and a lot of language that supports those who oppose tribal interests for whatever reason, but to place a client's interests on the slender reed of the Trilogy is no longer an option. In other words, read the Trilogy closely, but don't bring the Trilogy with you when you're facing [current] Chief Justice [John] Roberts. It is a useful thing for a student to know that advocacy is more than iterating precedent to the Court.

To return to the metaphor of the 200-year-old house described in Louise Erdrich's poem, *The Ritual*, the Marshall Trilogy houses the foundation of federal Indian law. This house's many rooms contain the various doctrines of law that form the substance of federal Indian law, but 200-year-old homes do not age well unless they are updated and retrofitted to include the newest improvements in housing technology. The house that is the Marshall Trilogy does not appear to have been improved. Instead, new rooms have been added to the core, a core that is still aging and rotting away. And no matter how nice the new rooms might be, it is always cold inside the core of that house, an iron cold of the deepest night.

> "[Marshall's] efforts to separate law
> from politics never entailed sacrificing
> legal rights in order to avoid political
> conflict."

The *Cherokee Nation* Ruling Was More a Legal than a Political Decision

Charles F. Hobson

Charles F. Hobson is a lecturer at the College of William and Mary and editor of The Papers of John Marshall. *In the following excerpt from his full-length biography of Marshall, Hobson considers the reasons for Marshall's decision in* Cherokee Nation v. Georgia. *The Marshall Court denied the Cherokee an injunction to prevent the state of Georgia from driving them off their land, deciding that the Court did not have jurisdiction to hear the case, since the Cherokee were not a foreign sovereign state, as they claimed. Hobson answers Marshall's critics by arguing that in* Cherokee *the chief justice sympathized with the Cherokee but made his opinions solely on legal considerations. In* Cherokee, *Hobson says, Marshall averted a political crisis by not hearing a case that could have had damaging political ramifications to the very authority of the fledgling judiciary but nonetheless did not sacrifice legal rights to achieve this end. Further, asserts Hobson, Marshall was not completely satisfied with the resolution of the case, which is why he requested that Justice Smith Thompson write the dissenting opinion that encouraged the Cherokee to bring another case to the Supreme Court the following year.*

The contradiction between natural law and positive law ... figured prominently in cases concerning the rights of the Cherokee Indians, which came before the Supreme Court in 1831 and 1882. Unlike slaves, Native Americans, though not citizens, enjoyed the status of free persons. They claimed not personal freedom but the right to remain in possession of their lands; and, in contrast to slaves who had only a natural right to freedom, their assertion of natural right also had a foundation in the Constitution and federal laws. Although the slave cases were uncontroversial and attracted little notice outside the courtroom, the Cherokee cases thrust the Supreme Court into the center of a partisan controversy that called into question once again the judiciary's role in the American polity. By merely agreeing to hear the cause of the Cherokees, the Court became a player in a political contest in which it was aligned with the opponents of the administration of President Andrew Jackson. In this awkward and uncomfortable position the Court faced the challenge of preserving its reputation as an impartial legal tribunal. Where legal rights were asserted and the Court had jurisdiction, however, Chief Justice Marshall was not one to shrink from controversy, insisting on the Court's duty to act no matter what the consequences. His efforts to separate law from politics never entailed sacrificing legal rights in order to avoid political conflict.

Background to the *Cherokee* Cases

The Cherokee cases originated in the hesitant and ambivalent Indian policy of the federal government, the constant push of white settlers upon Indian lands, and the aggressiveness of state governments impatient to assert their jurisdiction over remaining Indian lands lying within state boundaries. Empowered by the Constitution to regulate commerce with the Indian tribes and to make treaties for the purchase of Indian lands, the general government tried to follow an orderly policy of removing Indians beyond the pale of white settlement while guaranteeing title to their unceded lands. The assumption was that Indians were nomadic hunting peoples who could never be incorporated in "civilized" white society and that the tribes would accordingly continue to sell their lands as white settlement advanced.

In 1802 Georgia ceded its western lands to the United States in return for a promise that the federal government on behalf of the state would purchase all Indian lands within the state boundary as soon as possible and on reasonable terms. By the 1820s little progress had been made in extinguishing Indian titles. The Cherokees had taken up agriculture and refused to sell any more of their lands. In 1827 they adopted a constitution and declared themselves an independent state. In response Georgia enacted a series of laws seizing Cherokee territory, extending state law over this territory, and annulling all Indian customs and laws. These extreme actions encountered no opposition from the Jackson administration, which lent a sympathetic ear to assertions of state sovereignty, particularly in regard to Indian affairs. In 1830 the administration secured passage of the Indian Removal Act, by which the Indians could choose to remove west of the Mississippi River or submit to state law. In these circumstances the Cherokees, supported by well placed politicians and statesmen motivated both by genuine sympathy for the plight of the Indians and by desire to embarrass the administration, brought their cause to the Supreme Court. *Cherokee Nation v. Georgia* (1831) was an original action brought to restrain the state of Georgia from executing its laws in the Cherokee territory.

Indian Property Rights as Part of American Law

Until this case Marshall's most important statement about Indian rights occurred in *Johnson v. McIntosh* (1823), a land title dispute between white litigants, one of whom claimed under direct grants from Indians. The chief justice here elaborated a theory of an Indian "title of occupancy," a fully protected legal right that he distinguished from the discovering nation's "absolute ultimate title." Under this theory the government of the United States (which succeeded to rights of the British crown) had the exclusive right to extinguish (by purchase) the Indian title of occupancy and to convey absolute title in the soil to individuals. Such a title could not be acquired by direct purchase from Indians. *Johnson* defined an Indian right of property that attempted to bring traditional English property law in line with the actual circumstances governing relations between whites and Indians.... Marshall paid due homage to the principles of natural justice while grounding his decision largely in actual practice and positive law. Because of society's unquestioned right "to prescribe those rules by which property may be acquired and preserved," land titles necessarily depended "on the law of the nation" where the land lies. In resolving the case the Court therefore had to examine "not singly those principles of abstract justice, which the Creator of all things has impressed on the mind of his creature man, and which are admitted to regulate, in a great degree, the rights of civilized nations," but also the principles adopted by the American government for settling land disputes. In the resulting inquiry he left no doubt that Indian property rights were based not merely on "abstract justice" but firmly embedded in American law.

The British Crown's claim to absolute title in the soil of the North American continent, Marshall explained, was never asserted to deny the right of the original inhabitants to occupy the soil. This title was asserted, rather, against other European nations, who in order to avoid conflicts among themselves, adopted the principle of discovery. According to this principle, the discovering nation gained title "against all other European governments, which title might be consummated by possession." It gave to the discovering nation "the sole right of acquiring soil from the natives, and establishing settlements on it." The principle said nothing about relations between the discoverer and the native inhabitants, which "were to be regulated by themselves." As those relations developed, native rights "were, in no instance, entirely disregarded; but were necessarily, to a considerable extent, impaired." Their legal and just claim to occupy and retain possession of the soil was recognized, "but their rights to complete sovereignty, as independent nations, were necessarily diminished." In asserting their right of "ultimate dominion," European nations exercised the right to grant the soil even while it remained in possession of the natives. "These grants," said Marshall, "have been understood by all to convey a title to the grantees, subject only to the Indian right of occupancy," and he found abundant recognition of these principles in the historical record from discovery to the present.

The Crown's absolute title in the soil and exclusive right to extinguish the Indian right of occupancy was "incompatible with an absolute and complete title in the Indians." Admitting this state of affairs to have arisen largely through the superior force and arts of European civilization, Marshall sounded the theme he would [later] repeat. . . . Whether or not advanced civilizations had "a right, on abstract principles," to expel primitive hunting societies from their territory, conquest gave "a title which the courts of the conqueror cannot deny, whatever the private and speculative opinions of individuals may be, respecting the original justice of the claim which has been successfully asserted."

A Legal, Not Moral, Answer

As a pragmatic jurist, not a moralist, the chief justice was concerned only with finding the "legal" answer. Marshall was not entirely successful, however, in suppressing a tone of apology, even embarrassment, in discussing the fate of Native Americans. He spoke of the "pompous claims" of European nations to North America and the "extravagant . . . pretension of converting the discovery of an inhabited country into conquest." Since in fact the Europeans were able to sustain these fantastic assertions, he remarked somewhat abashedly, the principle that discovery conferred absolute title to the soil became "the law of the land." The same was true of the "concomitant principle" that Indians were "to be considered merely as occupants, to be protected, indeed, while in peace, in possession of their lands, but to be deemed incapable of transferring the absolute title to others." Such a restriction was contrary "to natural right, and to the usages of civilized nations," he ruefully admitted, but was nevertheless "indispensable" to the American system of settlement and "adapted to the actual condition of the two peoples." It could therefore, "perhaps, be supported by reason, and certainly cannot be rejected by courts of justice." Clearly, the chief justice experienced no little discomfort in announcing these principles as the law he had to apply to this case.

Still, the Indian right of occupancy was a recognized legal right of possession that was to be respected by American courts. Its subordinate status in the hierarchy of English common law, property right, moreover, was of little consequence to the Indian tribes. It did not matter to them that they could not convey absolute title. They were not restricted to selling their lands only to the federal government. They were perfectly free to sell land to individuals, including white persons, though the title conveyed was only the Indian title, the right of occupancy. This title would be held under the law of tribe, which retained power to annul the grant if it chose. If the tribe annulled the grant, said Marshall, "we know of no tribunal which can revise and set aside the proceeding." In the case at hand, the party's claim under an Indian grant was presumably defeated by the Indians themselves when they subsequently ceded their territory to the United States without reserving the particular tract.

In taking up the Cherokee cases, Chief Justice Marshall was thus on record in *Johnson v. McIntosh* as stating that Indian tribes had a legally protected right to their lands. They possessed not only property rights but also, he implied, rights of sovereignty as separate and distinct societies. Although not one to let his legal judgment be led astray by "feelings," Marshall expressed genuine sympathy for the cause of the Indians and indignation at the "disreputable" conduct of government towards them. The time had come, he wrote privately in 1828, "to give full indulgence to those principles of humanity and justice which ought always to govern our conduct towards the aborigines when this course can be pursued without exposing ourselves to the most afflicting calamities." Continued "oppression" of "a helpless people depending on our magnanimity and justice for the preservation of their existence, impresses a deep stain on the American character." The chief justice, we may be sure, was not displeased at having the opportunity to do as much as a jurist could do to remove this stain, especially when the denial of Indian rights occurred in consequence of an assertion of the noxious doctrine of state sovereignty.

The circumstances of *Cherokee Nation v. Georgia* counseled caution, however. The state of Georgia refused to appear in court and made clear its intention to ignore any decree the Supreme Court might issue directing the state to rescind its Cherokee laws. An equally important consideration was whether the executive department would enforce such a decree. Jackson's political opponents eagerly spread rumors that the president would ignore the Court's mandate. While no direct evidence could be cited to substantiate this charge, the president and his party did denounce these judicial proceedings as being part of a broader political campaign designed to unseat them in the election of 1832. Shortly before the case was argued, Congress debated a resolution to repeal section 25 of the Judiciary Act, which would have abolished the Supreme

Court's appellate review of state court decisions. In deciding on the legal rights of the Cherokees, the Marshall Court faced a direct challenge to its authority.

Marshall Appeases His Conscience

As it turned out, *Cherokee Nation v. Georgia* was not the case to consider the merits of the tribe's cause, for the Supreme Court ruled that it had no jurisdiction. As if to appease his conscience in having to deny the Indians a hearing, Marshall prefaced his opinion with a compassionate statement of their plea for justice that served as an implied censure of past government policy:

> If courts were permitted to indulge their sympathies, a case better calculated to excite them can scarcely be imagined. A people once numerous, powerful, and truly independent, found by our ancestors in the quiet and uncontrolled possession of an ample domain, gradually sinking beneath our superior policy, our arts, and our arms, have yielded their lands by successive treaties, each of which contains a solemn guarantee of the residue, until they retain no more of their formerly extensive territory than is deemed necessary to their comfortable subsistence. To preserve this remnant the present application is made.

To sustain jurisdiction it was necessary to show that the Cherokee tribe was a "foreign state" as that term was used in the jurisdiction clause of Article 3 of the Constitution. The chief justice was wholly persuaded that the Cherokees constituted a state, "a distinct political society, separated from others, capable of managing its own affairs and governing itself." At the same time, however, their territory lay within the jurisdictional limits of the United States, and in certain respects they were subject to its laws and acknowledged themselves to be under its protection. As he was wont to do when confronted with unsatisfactory alternatives, Marshall claimed the middle ground and fashioned his own unique solution. Indian tribes were neither independent foreign nations nor subject communities incorporated into the United States. They were "domestic dependent nations," whose relationship to the United States resembled that of a "ward to his guardian." In any event, it seemed clear that the framers did not mean to include Indians in conferring jurisdiction in disputes between a state and foreign states. This conclusion was supported as well by the language of the commerce clause, which explicitly distinguished Indian tribes from foreign nations.

Marshall also regarded as a serious objection to the jurisdiction that the bill of injunction sought relief beyond the Court's authority to act. It required the Court "to control the legislature of Georgia, and to restrain the exertion of its physical force." Such interposition was inappropriate, savoring "too much of the exercise of political power to be within the proper province of the judicial department." As far as remedying the wrongs committed against the Cherokee nation and securing the tribe against further injustice, the Supreme Court was "not the tribunal which can redress the past or prevent the future." Even on the matter of the Cherokees' claim to be protected in the possession of their lands, the Court could do nothing more perhaps than decide "the mere question of right . . . in a proper case with proper parties."

As in *Marbury v. Madison*, another case in which the assertion of legal right drew the judiciary department into conflict with the administration, the chief justice escaped an awkward dilemma by denying jurisdiction. In both instances the denial was the legally correct as well as a politically prudent decision. Although he averted a crisis that threatened the Court's authority, Marshall was not entirely satisfied with his resolution of the Cherokee case. In an extraordinary departure from his policy of preserving unity on the Court, he encouraged publication of a separate dissenting opinion. He also approved the court reporter's plan to publish the entire Cherokee case, including arguments of counsel, the dissenting opinion, and other materials that supported the tribe's claims. "As an individual I should be glad to see the whole case," wrote Marshall. "It is one in which a very narrow view has been taken in the opinion which is pronounced by the Court. The judge who pronounced that opinion [i.e., Marshall himself] had not time to consider the case in its various bearings; and had his time been so abundant, did not think it truly proper to pass the narrow limits that circumscribed the matter on which the decision of the court turned."

This publication, along with Marshall's hint about a "proper case with proper parties," encouraged the Cherokees and their friends to bring another case to the Supreme Court in 1832.

"We have found that Chief Justice Marshall . . . blatantly abused the plain language of the Constitution."

The Cherokee Were and Are a Sovereign Nation

Robert Yazzie

Robert Yazzie was chief justice of the Navajo Nation Supreme Court from 1992 to 2003. In the following essay, he and seven other Native American lawyers deliver a written opinion deciding the case of Cherokee Nation v. Georgia, *which was first heard in 1831 and reenacted in 1998 for an all-Indian mock Supreme Court. In the original case, chief justice John Marshall had denied the Cherokees' petition for an injunction against the state of Georgia, which the tribe claimed was restricting their rights and forcing them off their land. Marshall had concluded that the Supreme Court had no jurisdiction to hear the case because the Cherokee were not a sovereign foreign nation, as they claimed. In their opinion, Yazzie and the seven justices criticize Marshall's use of a technicality to avoid hearing "perhaps the most troublesome case in the history of the Court" but say that he addressed the fundamental question of what an Indian "nation" is. The Indian justices offer a history of Indian-colonist relations and show how, according to history, Indian nations were never part of the United States. They also assert that, according to previous treaties, the Cherokees' land rights should have been honored and protected. Justice Marshall, they conclude, was incorrect in his decision and that Indian Nations within the United States are in fact nations and states.*

Robert Yazzie, "Opinion: Cherokee Nation v. Georgia," *Kansas Journal of Law and Public Policy*, Vol. 8, Winter 1999. Copyright © 1999 *Kansas Journal of Law and Public Policy*. Reproduced by permission.

This appeal poses two issues which are of paramount importance to Indian nations *within* (although not part of) the United States and to the peoples of the American Republic: Is the Cherokee Nation of Indians a "foreign state" for the purposes of the exercise of original jurisdiction by the Supreme Court of the United States, and should American Indian nations continue to be regarded as "domestic dependent nations" of the United States? Of necessity, the just answer to these questions requires us to address basic principles of law, morality, and history. The discourse utilized in this opinion will primarily be that of the founders of the American Republic. Did the Federal Convention of 1787 intend to treat Indian nations as "foreign states" when it framed the Judicial Article? Given the sentiments of Europe toward "infidel princes" in the processes of crusade, conquest, and commerce, what is the true relation of Indian nations to the American state?

We will address these weighty questions by setting forth the jurisdiction of this Court, discussing the role of the Supreme Court of the United States in settling disputes between Indian nations and the States, and establishing the true nature of Indian nations. We will conclude by framing a proper conceptualization of Indian nations in a law based upon justice and humanity.

International Law Affirms Indian Rights

The justices of this Court are judges and lawyers who are members of Indian nations within the United States. This Court draws its legitimacy from the identities of its justices. They are members of the original nations of this continent. The justices bring many laws to this bench—the laws and legal traditions they learned in American law schools, and the laws of their own nations.

The law which governs here is international law. The founder of modern international law was Francisco de Vitoria, a 16th century Spanish law professor who wrote *De Indis et de*

Jure Belli Relectiones, or *On the Indians Lately Discovered.* It is the first international law text, and it clearly establishes the rights of Indians to their political liberty and to their lands. The ultimate conceit of what the American Bar Association calls "American Indian Affairs Law" lies in the fact that it is not the law *of* Indians. Non-Indians who sit in American legislatures and courts have no moral authority to unilaterally frame roles of law which establish or deny the rights of Indians. As Friar Antonio de Montesinos asked his congregation on Advent Sunday of 1511, "Tell me, by which right or justice do you keep these Indians in such a cruel and horrible servitude? On what authority have you waged a detestable war against these people? Are those not men? Have they not rational souls? Are you not bound to love them as you love yourselves?" . . .

The Nature of the Case Was Obscured

Was Chief Justice Marshall confused, or did he exercise sleight-of-hand to be rid of the Cherokee Nation? The opinion clearly mixes separate concepts laid out in article III, section 2 of the Constitution, judicial power and original jurisdiction. There are three paragraphs in section 2 which separately deal with judicial power, original jurisdiction, and the trial of crimes. The first paragraph enumerates the extent of judicial power by reciting the kinds of cases which fall under the Constitution and laws of the United States, including treaties. Marshall focused on the last category of cases which fall under the judicial power, "[suits] between a State, or the Citizens thereof, and foreign States, Citizens, or Subjects." The second paragraph sets out the original jurisdiction of the Supreme Court, including "those in which a State shall be a Party." The State of Georgia was a party. Alexander Hamilton explained, in *Federalist No. 81,* that "in cases in which a State might happen to be a party, it would ill suit its dignity to be turned over to an inferior tribunal," that was one reason for original jurisdiction in the Supreme Court.

This is a treaty case, and treaty disputes clearly fell under the judicial power set out in the first paragraph of article III, section 2. The State of Georgia was the defendant, and the second paragraph clearly gave original jurisdiction to hear the Cherokee petition. Blue smoke and mirrors obscured the nature of the case, and only Justices [Smith] Thompson and [Joseph] Story were able to find that Georgia's laws violated national law and treaties and say that an injunction should have been awarded.

What Is an Indian "Nation"?

Despite Chief Justice Marshall's use of a technicality to rid the Court of perhaps the most troublesome case in the history of the Court, he addressed a fundamental question of the time which is still relevant today—what *is* an Indian "nation"?

Without reviewing other statutes and policies prior to 1831 . . . evidence in the historical record shows that there was a consistent understanding that Indian nations were not considered to be a part of the United states; colonial, Confederation, or constitutional. The treaties with England of the period, British Indian policy, and the post-1763 policy which developed in the emerging United States of America all made it clear that Indians and their nations possessed rights to political liberty and property (land) which could not be taken except by trade, treaty, or war.

Chief Justice Marshall used international law to develop his dictum about "dependent domestic nations." At the time, international law was part of the core curriculum for law students and the writings of [Swiss philosopher Emmerich de] Vattel and [Dutch jurist Hugo] Grotius were well known. They restated what Francisco de Vitoria said in the first international law text, that Indians, as humans, possessed rights to their political liberty and their lands. As [George] Washington and others noted, the basic thrust of United States Indian policy was to acquire lands from Indians by purchase rather than war. War is the subject of international law, as are treaties. It was a fiction to state that Indian nations were "dependent," because the Indian Commerce Clause addressed Indian nations that were both within and without the jurisdiction of the United States. In 1831, the United States had not yet acquired Texas (1845), Oregon Territory (1846) or the Mexican territories (1848). With the exception of Louisiana (1812) and Missouri (1821), the remainder of the Louisiana Purchase was unorganized, and it was full of Indian nations with whom future treaties would have to be negotiated. To the extent that Indian nations allied themselves with the United States by treaty, such as the Cherokee Treaty of 1785, the "dependent" relationship might apply. Dependent states are defined as follows: "Foreign control of the affairs of a state may occur under a title of international law, for example as a consequence of a treaty of protection, or some other form of consent to agency or representation in external relations, or of a lawful war of collective defence and sanction leading to an occupation of the aggressor and imposition of measures designed to remove the sources of aggression." The Cherokee Treaty of 1785 was such a "treaty of protection" because the Cherokee Nation agreed to ally itself with the United States by treaty and permit the United States to conduct foreign affairs with other nations. The definition assumes consent, freely given. The problem with Marshall's dictum is that he swept all Indian nations into the same category, ignoring the fact that dependent nation status depends upon consent.

Cherokee and States' Rights

We have found that Chief Justice Marshall's analysis in *The Cherokee Case* was incorrect in terms of the understandings of the time. He blatantly abused the plain language of the Constitution in ruling that the Supreme Court did not have original jurisdiction over the case. At end, however, we must address the question which has lingered from initial occupation by Europeans to the present: What *are* Indian "nations"? What should they be? Even if one agrees that as of at least 1831 Indian nations had international status as states, is it realistic to have such a status in this day and age?

At end, we must return to the humanist roots of Indian policy. While [American jurist] Felix S. Cohen wrote that positive humanist principles are at the root of American Indian law, they are irrelevant in today's corpus of Indian law. There is no "real equality of the races" in any meaningful sense. Court decisions are not race-based, in that the courts rule in favor of one race over another, but it is clear that where a State or a corporation is a litigant, there is no such equality. The principle of tribal self-government is eroded by rulings dealing with criminal jurisdiction over non-Indians and nonmember Indians, civil jurisdiction over nonmembers, and a definition of Indian country which undermines self-government. *The Cherokee Case* was the start of the "States rights" movement which led to the Civil War. Today, States rights so drives federal Indian law as to vitiate the principle of "Federal sovereignty in Indian affairs." Despite invitations to Congress by the Supreme Court to use its legislative powers to change things, when that happens, courts deny even that "plenary" power. Finally, the "principle of governmental protection of Indians" is largely meaningless. The very officials whose duty it is to "protect" Indian nations are often the first to compromise to the detriment of those they are obligated to protect.

Indian Nations Are States

We hold that the Indian Nations *within* (and not "of") the United States are nations and states. We further hold that an Indian nation cannot revert to dependent state status in the absence of a treaty with the United States, negotiated at arms-length with meaningful Indian nation consent, and followed with utmost good faith. We hold that existing treaties can and should be modified or amended and that Indian nations must have a treaty with the United States if it is to be considered a "dependent" nation.

We hold that Indian peoples have survived *as* Indians in communities, and they shall continue to do so in the future.

This cause is remanded to the Supreme Court of the United States with instructions to assume jurisdiction over the underlying cause and to enter an injunction in favor of the Cherokee Nation, and to enforce it, even if that requires mobilization of the Army, as was done when the Court entered civil rights decrees in the Fifties and Sixties.

CHAPTER 2

Upholding Congressional
Power over Tribes

Case Overview

Lone Wolf v. Hitchcock (1903)

In 1867, Lone Wolf, chief of the Kiowa people, joined other southern Great Plains tribes to sign a treaty with the U.S. government. Under the terms of the Treaty of Medicine Lodge Creek, as it was known, the Kiowa and Comanche gave up 90 million acres of their land in exchange for a 2.9-million-acre reservation in Western Oklahoma. By a subsequent treaty, the Apache were also to live on this reservation land. Medicine Lodge Creek provided that no more land could be sold or given away without the consent of three-quarters of the adult male members of the tribes. In 1887, Congress passed the General Allotment Act, also known as the Dawes Act, authorizing the president to allot tribal land to individual Native Americans. In 1892, the Jerome Commission obtained consent from tribe members, and reservation lands were subsequently broken up into privately owned parcels of property.

Almost immediately, American Indian representatives claimed that assent to selling the lands had been obtained fraudulently by government agents and that three-quarters of the adult males had not agreed to cede the land. The United States House of Representatives ignored the Indians' appeals, voting to execute the agreement, but the bill was defeated in the Senate in January 1899. But then in early 1900, Congress passed an act allowing the government access to the disputed land. After allotting some of the land to individuals and setting parcels aside for common use, the federal government was free to purchase the "remaining" land.

Lone Wolf challenged the act's constitutionality and took Ethan Hitchcock of the Department of the Interior to court. The Kiowa hired William McKendree Springer to litigate their case. Springer argued before a federal court that the act violated the tribes' property rights and that the Indians had been denied their due-process rights. Springer lost in two lower courts before appealing to the United States Supreme Court and rearguing the case in 1902. He lost again. The unanimous decision in *Lone Wolf v. Hitchcock* was handed down on January 5, 1903.

Associate Justice Edward White of Louisiana wrote the decision. His remarks led *Lone Wolf* to later be referred to as "the Indian *Dred Scott*," (the 1856 Supreme Court decision denying African Americans citizenship), and January 5, 1903, to be regarded as "one of the blackest days in the history of the American Indians." In his remarks, White called the Native Americans "ignorant and dependent," "weak and diminishing in number," and "wards of the nation" and ruled that Congress possessed absolute authority over Native American property "by reason of its exercise of guardianship over their interests." White also held that the congressional act represented only "a mere change in the form of investment of Indian tribal property from land to money," even though the Cherokee argued that the land was obtained fraudulently. He said that Congress had made a good-faith effort to compensate the Kiowa for their lands, and thus the Fifth Amendment had not been violated.

Lone Wolf made it impossible for Native Americans to seek redress from the courts after their land had been taken away and treaties nullified. The next five decades saw American Indians forcibly separated from their land, and their way of life and their communities eroded. Finally, in 1955, the Indian Claims Commission awarded the Kiowa, Comanche, and Apache $2 million in compensation for the lands taken under the congressional act of 1900.

> "The power exists to abrogate the provisions of an Indian treaty."

The Court's Decision: Congress Can Repeal Any Treaty with the Indians

Edward D. White

Edward D. White was a senator from Louisiana who was appointed to the Supreme Court in 1894. From 1910 until his death in 1921 he served as the Court's ninth chief justice. In his written opinion in the case of Lone Wolf v. Hitchcock, *White spoke for a unanimous Court, holding that Congress has plenary, or absolute, power over Native American property and may dispose of it at its discretion. In 1900, Congress passed an act that allowed the United States to take title to 2.9 million acres of the Kiowa, Comanche, and Plains Apache reservation in Oklahoma. The Kiowa chief, Lone Wolf, took Ethan Hitchcock, secretary of the interior, to court for violating the 1867 Medicine Lodge Creek Treaty. That treaty, signed with the Kiowa and Comanche, relinquished Indian claims to 90 million acres in exchange for the 2.9 million acres in question. White's decision uses condescending language to speak of Native Americans, calling them "ignorant," "weak," and "wards of the nation." He held that Congress had complete authority over Indian land because of the guardian-ward relationship. Because of their power as guardians of tribes, Congress could abrogate provisions of treaties with them. White also argued that the congressional act of 1900 represented only "a mere change in the form of investment of In-*

Edward D. White, majority opinion, *Lone Wolf v. Hitchcock*, U.S. Supreme Court, 187 U.S. 553 (1903).

dian tribal property from land to money," even though the
Cherokee argued that the land was obtained fraudulently and
taken for below market value. White's decision has been characterized as the "Indian's Dred Scott *decision,*" (the 1856 Supreme
Court decision denying African Americans citizenship), and
January 5, 1903, has been called "one of the blackest days in the
history of the American Indians."

By the sixth article of the first of the two treaties ... proclaimed on August 25, 1868, it was provided that heads of
families of the tribes affected by the treaty might select, within
the reservation, a tract of land of not exceeding 320 acres in
extent, which should thereafter cease to be held in common,
and should be for the exclusive possession of the Indian making the selection so long as he or his family might continue to
cultivate the land. The twelfth article reads as follows:

> Article 12. No treaty for the cession of any portion or part
> of the reservation herein described, which may be held in
> common, shall be of any validity or force, as against the said
> Indians, unless executed and signed by at least three fourths
> of all the adult male Indians occupying the same, and no
> cession by the tribe shall be understood or construed in
> such manner as to deprive, without his consent, any indi-
> vidual member of the tribe of his rights to any tract of land
> selected by him as provided in article 3 of this treaty.

The appellants base their right to relief on the proposition
that by the effect of the article just quoted the confederated
tribes of Kiowas, Comanches, and Apaches were vested with
an interest in the lands held in common within the reservation, which interest could not be devested by Congress in
any other mode than that specified in the said twelfth article,
and that as a result of the said stipulation the interest of
the Indians in the common lands fell within the protection
of the 5th Amendment to the Constitution of the United
States, and such interest—indirectly at least—came under the

control of the judicial branch of the government. We are unable to yield our assent to this view.

The Dependent Status of Indians

The contention in effect ignores the status of the contracting Indians and the relation of dependency they bore and continue to bear towards the government of the United States. To uphold the claim would be to adjudge that the indirect operation of the treaty was to materially limit and qualify the controlling authority of Congress in respect to the care and protection of the Indians, and to deprive Congress, in a possible emergency, when the necessity might be urgent for a partition and disposal of the tribal lands, of all power to act, if the assent of the Indians could not be obtained.

Now, it is true that in decisions of this court, the Indian right of occupancy of tribal lands, whether declared in a treaty or otherwise created, has been stated to be sacred, or, as sometimes expressed, as sacred as the fee of the United States in the same lands. *Johnson v. M'Intosh* (1823), *Cherokee Nation v. Georgia* (1831), *Worcester v. Georgia* (1832), *United States v. Cook* (1873) *Leavenworth, L. & G. R. Co. v. United States* (1875), *Beecher v. Wetherby* (1877). But in none of these cases was there involved a controversy between Indians and the government respecting the power of Congress to administer the property of the Indians. The questions considered in the cases referred to, which either directly or indirectly had relation to the nature of the property rights of the Indians, concerned the character and extent of such rights as respected states or individuals. In one of the cited cases it was clearly pointed out that Congress possessed a paramount power over the property of the Indians, by reason of its exercise of guardianship over their interests, and that such authority might be implied, even though opposed to the strict letter of a treaty with the Indians. Thus, in *Beecher v. Wetherby*, discussing the claim that there had been a prior reservation of land by treaty to the use of a certain tribe of Indians, the court said:

> But the right which the Indians held was only that of occupancy. The fee was in the United States, subject to that right, and could be transferred by them whenever they chose. The grantee it is true, would take only the naked fee, and could not disturb the occupancy of the Indians; that occupancy could only be interfered with or determined by the United States. It is to be presumed that in this matter the United States would be governed by such considerations of justice as would control a Christian people in their treatment of an ignorant and dependent race. Be that as it may, the propriety or justice of their action towards the Indians with respect to their lands is a question of governmental policy, and is not a matter open to discussion in a controversy between third parties, neither of whom derives title from the Indians.

Congress Has Had Absolute Power

Plenary authority over the tribal relations of the Indians has been exercised by Congress from the beginning, and the power has always been deemed a political one, not subject to be controlled by the judicial department of the government. Until the year 1871 the policy was pursued of dealing with the Indian tribes by means of treaties, and, of course, a moral obligation rested upon Congress to act in good faith in performing the stipulations entered into on its behalf. But, as with treaties made with foreign nations, the legislative power might pass laws in conflict with treaties made with the Indians.

The power exists to abrogate the provisions of an Indian treaty, though presumably such power will be exercised only when circumstances arise which will not only justify the government in disregarding the stipulations of the treaty, but may demand, in the interest of the country and the Indians themselves, that it should do so. When, therefore, treaties were entered into between the United States and a tribe of Indians it was never doubted that the power to abrogate existed in Congress, and that in a contingency such power might be availed of from considerations of governmental policy, particularly if consistent with perfect good faith towards the Indians. In *United States v. Kagama* (1885) speaking of the Indians, the court said:

> After an experience of a hundred years of the treaty-making system of government Congress has determined upon a new departure—to govern them by acts of Congress. This is seen in the act of March 3, 1871, embodied in 2079 of the Revised Statutes: 'No Indian nation or tribe, within the territory of the United States, shall be acknowledged or recognized as an independent nation, tribe, or power with whom the United States may contract by treaty; but no obligation of any treaty lawfully made and ratified with any such Indian nation or tribe prior to March 3d, 1871, shall be hereby invalidated or impaired.

In upholding the validity of an act of Congress which conferred jurisdiction upon the courts of the United States for certain crimes committed on an Indian reservation within a state, the court said 'It seems to us that this is within the competency of Congress. These Indian tribes are the wards of the nation. They are communities dependent on the United States. Dependent largely for their daily food. Dependent for their political rights. They own no allegiance to the states, and receive from them no protection. Because of the local ill feeling, the people of the states where they are found are often their deadliest enemies. From their very weakness and helplessness, so largely due to the course of dealing of the Federal government with them and the treaties in which it has been promised, there arises the duty of protection, and with it the power. This has always been recognized by the executive and by Congress, and by this court, whenever the question has arisen.

Congress Acted in Good Faith

> The power of the general government over these remnants
> of a race once powerful, now weak and diminished in num-
> bers, is necessary to their protection, as well as to the safety
> of those among whom they dwell. It must exist in that gov-
> ernment, because it never has existed anywhere else, because
> the theater of its exercise is within the geographical limits of
> the United States, because it has never been denied, and be-
> cause it alone can enforce its laws on all the tribes.

That Indians who had not been fully emancipated from the
control and protection of the United States are subject, at least
so far as the tribal lands were concerned, to be controlled by
direct legislation of Congress, is also declared in *Choctaw Nation v. United States* and *Stephens v. Choctaw Nation*.

In view of the legislative power possessed by Congress
over treaties with the Indians and Indian tribal property, we
may not specially consider the contentions pressed upon our
notice that the signing by the Indians of the agreement of October 6, 1892, was obtained by fraudulent misrepresentations,
and concealment, that the requisite three fourths of adult
male Indians had not signed, as required by the twelfth article
of the treaty of 1867, and that the treaty as signed had been
amended by Congress without submitting such amendments
to the action of the Indians since all these matters, in any
event, were solely within the domain of the legislative authority, and its action is conclusive upon the courts.

The act of June 6, 1900, which is complained of in the bill,
was enacted at a time when the tribal relations between the
confederated tribes of Kiowas, Comanches, and Apaches still
existed, and that statute and the statutes supplementary thereto
dealt with the disposition of tribal property, and purported to
give an adequate consideration for the surplus lands not allot-
ted among the Indians or reserved for their benefit. Indeed,
the controversy which this case presents is concluded by the
decision in *Cherokee Nation v. Hitchcock*, decided at this term,

where it was held that full administrative power was possessed by Congress over Indian tribal property. In effect, the action of Congress now complained of was but an exercise of such power, a mere change in the form of investment of Indian tribal property, the property of those who as we have held, were in substantial effect the wards of the government. We must presume that Congress acted in perfect good faith in the dealings with the Indians of which complaint is made, and that the legislative branch of the government exercised its best judgment in the premises. In any event, as Congress possessed full power in the matter, the judiciary cannot question or inquire into the motives which prompted the enactment of this legislation. If injury was occasioned, which we do not wish to be understood as implying, by the use made by Congress of its power, relief must be sought by an appeal to that body for redress, and not to the courts. The legislation in question was constitutional, and the demurrer to the bill was therefore rightly sustained.

The motion to dismiss does not challenge jurisdiction over the subject-matter. Without expressly referring to the propositions of fact upon which it proceeds, suffice it to say that we think it need not be further adverted to, since, for the reasons previously given and the nature of the controversy, we think the decree . . . should be affirmed.

"Lone Wolf's legacy lies not so much in the legal doctrine that bears his name, but in the dogged refusal to admit defeat that still characterizes native advocates."

Lone Wolf's Legacy Is His Perseverance

Ann Laquer Estin

Ann Laquer Estin is a professor of law at the University of Iowa. In the following essay, she discusses the details of Lone Wolf v. Hitchcock, *focusing on the events that led up to the case and its decision. She describes the cold reception of the Kiowa chief when he went to Washington to criticize the terms of the Jerome Allottment that forced Indians to sell off portions of their land and press for the return of property that had been unfairly appropriated by the United States government. Estin explains how the Indians faced an uphill legal battle, detailing the obstacles they faced in their suit against the federal government and arguing that the entire episode was orchestrated to ensure Indian failure. Estin maintains that the effect of* Lone Wolf *was to make clear that tribal property rights were subject to change at the whim of the legislative branch of government. But she points out that the decision also affected a spirit of advocacy among Indian lobbyists in their refusal to admit defeat by the federal government for injustices done.*

Ann Laquer Estin, *The Aggressions of Civilization: Federal Indian Policy Since the 1880's*. Philadelphia: Temple University Press, 1984, pp. 215–45. Edited by Sandra L. Cadwalader and Vine Deloria. Copyright © 1984 by Temple University. All rights reserved. Reproduced by permission of the editors.

When Commissioner of Indian Affairs J.D.C. Atkins arrived at the Kiowa, Comanche, and Kiowa-Apache reservation during the winter of 1886–1887, his purpose was to enlist Indian support for the allotment acts pending in Congress. Sponsored by Senator Henry L. Dawes and other reform-minded congressmen and organizations, the acts were intended to divide tribal lands into small homestead-sized farming tracts and distribute them to the Indians. The reformers believed that the ownership of their own lands would transform the Indians into a modern agricultural people, separate from their tribal past.

Instead of gaining enthusiastic Indian support, Commissioner Atkins encountered the "determined opposition" of the southern plains tribes; his visit in fact spurred the Indian leaders into action. Defying efforts by the local agent to keep them on their reservation, Lone Wolf of the Kiowas and Chief Jake of the Caddos traveled by train to Washington to fight the proposed legislation. Lone Wolf and Chief Jake arrived too late; the General Allotment Act had been passed on February 8, 1887. The two Indians demanded to see Commissioner Atkins, and then returned home to Indian territory to rally the tribes against the policy.

For Lone Wolf, called Guipagho by the Kiowa, the fruitless trip to Washington marked the start of a long fight to protect his tribe's land and community. His unrelenting efforts won him the enmity of a succession of Indian agents and commissioners, but he persisted for more than fifteen years against increasingly impossible odds. Lone Wolf's final defeat came at the hands of the Supreme Court in *Lone Wolf v. Hitchcock* (1903), his suit to enjoin the allotment of the tribe's reservation.

The Kiowa, Comanche, and Apache reservation has long since disappeared into Oklahoma history, but the Court's decision in *Lone Wolf v. Hitchcock* has remained a cornerstone of federal Indian law. The case is still cited frequently for its principal holding: that Congress has plenary power to abrogate the terms of Indian treaties. As a legal doctrine, the plenary power rule has prevented the courts from reviewing federal Indian legislation, effectively leaving the tribes at the mercy of shifting congressional moods and majorities. Although based on the idea that Congress acts as a guardian for the nation's dependent Indian wards, the rule's function is to facilitate continued congressional appropriation of tribal lands and resources.

Both in Congress and before the Supreme Court, the Kiowas were assisted in their efforts by the Indian Rights Association. Despite its firm support for the goals of allotment policy, the Association insisted that tribal consent was essential whenever Congress tried to modify the terms of Indian treaties; it believed that a great injustice had been done the Kiowas. It was also clear to the Association (after several decades of involvement in Indian policy) that Congress could not be trusted to consider fairly the interest of Indian communities. After the Court's ruling, the Association editorialized:

> It is now distinctly understood that Congress has a right to do as it pleases; that it is under no obligation to respect any treaty, for Indians have no rights which command respect. What is to be hoped for by an appeal to Congress can readily be anticipated by the history of the legislation by which Lone Wolf and his tribe have been deprived of that which had by express treaty stipulation apparently been secured to them. . . .

The Jerome Agreement

The tribes proposed an alternative to the Jerome agreement, asking that if they could not "be granted the privilege of keeping our reservation," that a new treaty be made which would provide sufficient land to graze cattle. The memorial also pointed out that the tribes were making a good-faith effort to conform to the demands of the new order.

[W]e are not drunkards, nor do we molest the property of the whites who have located on lands adjoining ours. We have placed our children in schools provided by the Government and Christian societies ... these several schools, having a capacity for 700 pupils, are kept filled with our children. ... [W]e point to these facts as evidence that we are striving in the right ways to fit our people for the day we realize must come, when their children will be dependent upon their own intelligence and physical strength for the support of themselves and their kindred.

At the same time the Kiowas, Comanches, and Apaches were drafting their petition to Congress, the whites located around the reservation borders began collecting affidavits to submit to the Senate. The testimony compiled from hundred of eager boomers sought primarily to rebut the argument that the land was unfit for farming.

The legislative debate had by this point shifted from the issue of allotment and opening the reservation to a battle over acreage. Under the original Jerome agreement, the tribes would have been permitted to keep only 453,000 acres, or about 15 percent of their reservation land. The IRA [Indian Rights Association] and Interior Department proposals to grant larger allotments meant there would be less land available for non-Indian settlement; these revisions were stridently opposed by the "boomers."

In February 1900, the House proponents of ratification tried a new approach, and added their two-year-old bill as a rider to another Senate Indian bill that concerned the Fort Hall Reservation in Idaho. After the amended Fort Hall bill passed the House, it returned to the Senate, where Senator O.H. Platt of Connecticut, a loyal sympathizer of the Indian Rights Association, requested a conference on the amendment. Platt lost his bid to stop the legislation, however, and the bill passed the Senate without debate at the end of the session. No words in the title of the Act of June 6, 1900 indicated that

Section VI was a ratification of the long-disputed Jerome agreement. The ratification legislation amended the original Jerome agreement in several critical ways, but the amendments were never submitted to the three tribes for their approval.

The legislative history of the ratification demonstrates that the interests of the tribes were sacrificed for a politically expedient result. Congress had been clearly informed that the tribes did not consent to the terms of the agreement: even if the number of initial signatures were sufficient, the "agreement" was repudiated time and again by the members of the tribes, eventually by a greater number than had originally signed.

For almost seven years the Indian Rights Association, architects and firm supporters of allotment, had worked to block ratification because it was against the interests of the tribes. The Association's opposition came both from a practical assessment—that the allotments were too small to be successful—and from the principle that the tribes' treaty required their consent before federal legislation could modify the Indians' property rights.

Proponents of the bill were hardly without influential friends; the "boomers" in Kansas and the Oklahoma Territory found a powerful ally in the railroads. For decades, the railroad lobby had posed a serious threat to tribal rights and interests, and different Indian nations had already suffered substantial legislative defeats at their hands. For the Kiowas, Comanches, and Apaches, the story was no different. After losing the Senate fight, Samuel Brosius, Washington agent for the Indian Rights Association, commented that the bill had been railroaded through Congress, adding: "The word 'railroad' is used advisedly, since it is chiefly by reason of the efforts of the Chicago, Rock Island and Pacific railroad officers that the legislation was secured."

Lone Wolf Files Suit

A month after Congress ratified the revised Jerome agreement, a delegation from the three tribes visited Washington to argue for a better bill. The group met briefly with President [William] McKinley, but were informed that the matter would not be reconsidered. Once convinced that the bill would not be repealed, the tribes split again into factions. Lone Wolf and [Comanche leader] Eschiti were aligned with a group of Kiowas and Comanches unwilling to concede defeat, while [Comanche chief] Quanah Parker, [Kiowa leader] Apiatan, and [Apache leader] Apache John resigned themselves to allotment and fell in line as the officially recognized "principal chiefs" of the three tribes.

It is hardly surprising that a leader like Quanah chose to acquiesce once allotment had been ratified. Much of his power and prestige was based on his ability to exploit the essentially colonial system of the reservation. From the Texas cattlemen through a whole string of Indian agents, Quanah's cooperation and his ability to bring his many followers around had been richly rewarded.

It is less clear why Lone Wolf and Eschiti chose to risk their status as tribal leaders by continuing to oppose allotment. Cooperation with the federal bureaucracy had already become a sort of litmus test for tribal leadership, with the federal government in a strong position to select and support the "chiefs" among the tribes. One common method was to appoint some tribal leaders to special positions: Lone Wolf, Quanah, and White Man sat as judges on the reservation's Indian Court from 1886 to 1901, and were paid a salary of $10 per month.

Perhaps because they had no leader like Quanah Parker, the Kiowas had not been as cooperative as the Comanches. Or perhaps stronger feelings among the Kiowas led Lone Wolf to become a different sort of leader. In any event, his efforts to block allotment earned Lone Wolf the enormous hostility of the agent, James Randlett, and before long he lost his status as a principal chief of the Kiowas.

When Lone Wolf arrived with a delegation in Washington in June 1901, after retaining former congressman and federal judge William Springer as an attorney, his reception was none too warm. Springer wrote on June 23 to the Indian Rights Association requesting funds to pay the Indians' way home. Springer wrote, "Secretary [of the interior Ethan] Hitchcock will not recognize the delegates who have come to Washington to avert this outrage, and nine full blood Kiowas and Comanches are now here without money or means to return to their reservation."

Matthew K. Sniffen quickly responded that the Association would be glad to send a committee member to see Hitchcock and President McKinley. The next day, however, Sniffen received a letter from Francis E. Leupp, a journalist who had served as the Association's Washington agent. Leupp wrote in confidence, urging that the Association act cautiously so far as Springer was concerned; he suggested that the lawyer was down on his luck and short of funds.

Later the same week, N. Dubois Miller of the Association wrote to Secretary Hitchcock to ask for a clarification of the situation. The Secretary's prompt response reflected both Leupp's skepticisms and Lone Wolf's fading status. Hitchcock stated that he had twice received the delegation, but only unofficially. "This so-called delegation," wrote Hitchcock, "was wholly unauthorized to come here by his tribe." Hitchcock also commented that Springer had afterward attempted to collect a substantial fee for representing the Indians.

Springer had filed a complaint for Lone Wolf in the equity division of the Supreme Court of the District of Columbia on June 6, naming Hitchcock a defendant. The suit sought to restrain the Interior Department from carrying out the provisions of the allotment act, arguing that the acts of Congress were "unconstitutional and void" and a violation of "solemn treaty provisions." On June 17, Springer amended the bill of complaint to include seven additional Indians as plaintiffs, and stated that the eight had been authorized to act as delegates of the three tribes at a general council held at Anadarko from June 3 to June 7.

In a ruling handed down on June 20, the court denied a preliminary injunction and rejected Springer's contention that the acts deprived the tribes of their property without due process of law. The opinion by Justice A.C. Bradley in *Lone Wolf v. Hitchcock* described the history of the allotment legislation as "the usual process," and held that misunderstanding, deception, and lack of tribal consent were not relevant to the court's determination, the matter being one for exclusive consideration by Congress. As for the process due the tribes in Congress, "It is to be assumed that they [the tribes' objections] were carefully considered and determined with due regard to the public interests of and the rights of the Indian."

On June 26, Springer appealed the court's final decree, but by the time the Court of Appeals heard the case the opening of the Kiowa, Comanche, and Apache reservation was an accomplished fact. By proclamation of President McKinley on July 4, 1901, the date of opening was set for August 6, 1901. . . .

A Foregone Conclusion

Before Lone Wolf's appeal reached the Supreme Court, the trap was set and ready to spring shut. [Hampton L.] Carson and Springer attempted both in their brief and in their oral argument to draw a line between political matters and property rights, urging that Congress had plenary power only where political questions were concerned.

Springer and Carson argued in their brief in *Lone Wolf* that tribal consent was required by the treaties and the Dawes Act, and called the taking of land from the Indians without their consent "an act without a precedent." To explain why the tribes' property rights should be respected when other tribal rights had been held abrogable, the lawyers argued that the Indians' treaty-recognized title was a vested property right, bringing it under the rule that legislative acts impairing vested rights are unconstitutional.

The formalist argument was in the tradition of nineteenth-century property law, where the protection accorded any interest was capsulized in the legal label used to characterize it. Springer and Carson disputed the appeals court's labeling of the tribes as "tenants at will" of the United States; rather, they insisted that Supreme Court decisions had identified the tribes as "life tenants," the latter being a freehold estate, one of the magic words which brought it to the level of vested property right.

[Assistant attorney general Willis] Van Devanter's brief relied on the recent precedent and a straightforward argument: that Indians were wards of the government, that treaty-making was a political function, and that the Court had already upheld congressional "administration" of Indian property by direct legislative enactment. For good measure, the government brief pointed out that whether Congress had ever taken tribal land without tribal consent did not answer the question of its power to do so, and argued that the Indians had consented to the act as passed by accepting their allotments. Van Devanter also disputed the characterization of the Indian right of occupancy that the appellants developed, and argued further that the three tribes had not been deprived of their property; rather, there had been merely a change in the form of the assets, from land to money.

Oral argument was held on October 23, 1902, with Springer and Carson sharing the duties. Springer wrote to Matthew Sniffen of the Association two weeks later with glowing praise for Carson's "clear and eloquent" closing argument and an optimistic assessment of the result. Samuel Brosius wrote to Sniffen with the same enthusiasm, relating the account of an attorney who had heard Carson's argument and called it "the finest he had ever heard" before the Supreme Court, with the Court "a unit in paying Carson the closest attention." Brosius' acquaintance reported that the justices were "listless even to rudeness" during Van Devanter's argument, and "kept propounding questions to show they did not agree."

Brosius' optimism proved unfounded, however; when the Supreme Court issued its opinion on January 5, 1903, the decision fit squarely in line with the preceding cases.

> We must presume that Congress acted in perfect good faith in dealing with the Indians of which complaint is made ... In any event, as Congress possessed full power in the matter, the judiciary cannot question or inquire into the motives which prompted enactment of this legislation. If injury was occasioned, which we do not wish to be understood as implying, by the use made of Congress of its power, relief must be sought by an appeal to that party for redress and not to the courts.

This ingenuous suggestion that the tribes appeal to Congress for relief shields the harsher truth evident in the facts before the Court in Lone Wolf's case. Since the tribes had used every possible means over a period of almost eight years to prevent passage of a ratification bill, their hope of "relief" from Congress was clearly meaningless.

In this context, the full import of *Lone Wolf v. Hitchcock* was immediately clear: all aspects of tribal political and property rights were now subject to radical changes at the whim of the legislative branch. At best, tribes might retain rights only so long as more powerful political pressure-groups had no interest in their Indian resources and no objection to their continued existence.

The final defeat of Indian rights in the courts was assessed by the Indian Rights Association at an executive committee meeting two days after the decision. The minutes of the meeting report that [IRA cofounder] "Mr. [Herbert] Welsh suggested that in view of the uniformly unfavorable decision rendered on the Indian cases—which have cost a great deal of money—the Association ought to be very cautious about further appeals to the courts.

The denial of judicial remedies created urgent new business in Washington for groups like the Association. In the next session of Congress, Senators and Representatives from western states moved to implement the broad power accorded them by the Court, and the "Friends of the Indian" scrambled to convince Congress of its "moral obligation." The Association was particularly active in fighting measures to allot the Rosebud Sioux reservation and to appropriate Chippewa timber resources.

Both of these bills were eventually defeated, but the hectic round of lobbying set the pattern for the future. With no possibility of judicial reversal, every legislative battle to fend off treaty abrogation became crucially important. Without representation as tribes in Congress, and without the wealth required to support massive lobbies on their behalf, Indians have no assurance even today that their fundamental interests in property and political autonomy will be respected or even considered in Congress.

Refusal to Admit Defeat

Lone Wolf's legacy lies not so much in the legal doctrine that bears his name, but in the dogged refusal to admit defeat that still characterizes native advocates who must deal with the federal government. The cast of characters has changed—today's uphill legislative battles are fought each term by Indian lobbyists, such as the representatives of the National Congress of American Indians or the Native American Rights Fund—but the problem remains the same.

Three-quarters of a century after *Lone Wolf*, the contours of the plenary power doctrine remain largely intact. Recent developments in federal Indian law have blunted some of the sharper outrages of the plenary power rule; several Supreme

Court opinions have undermined the theory that Indian affairs are unreviewable as a type of "political question," and the Court has in a few cases scrutinized federal Indian legislation on constitutional grounds. Ironically, although the plenary power rule of *Lone Wolf* continues to stand, the argument made by Carson and Springer has been vindicated: treaty-recognized property rights are now legally distinguished from the "right of occupancy" of aboriginal title, and in a limited range of cases treaty title to property is now considered sufficiently vested to be protected by the Fifth Amendment.

Despite these modest doctrinal advances, the courts continue to accord Congress the authority to regulate the internal affairs of Indian tribes and the power to abrogate venerable treaty obligations. New bills are introduced in each Congress seeking to legislate away Indian treaty provisions, and despite occasional successes in the courts, Indian tribes still cannot rely on judicial review for protection against congressional assaults on their tribal property and governments.

> *"[Justice White displayed] a lucid and self-contradictory ability to rewrite history in a way that legitimized congressional power over tribes."*

The *Lone Wolf* Decision Damaged Tribal Sovereignty

David Eugene Wilkins

David E. Wilkins is a professor of American Indian studies, political science, law, and American Studies at the University of Minnesota. In the following article, he provides historical background to the Lone Wolf v. Hitchcock *case, beginning from the Treaty of Medicine Lodge in 1867 that created distinct reservation boundaries and gave Indians rights to a specific portion of land. Wilkins describes how the U.S. government sought to appropriate that land, despite the treaty, and how the Kiowa chief Lone Wolf filed suit to retain Indian rights to the property. The treaty and constitutional arguments presented by the Indians' lawyers, while compelling, Wilkins says, were overshadowed by the U.S. attorney's views of Indians as "wards" who were fully controlled by Congress. Wilkins concludes that Justice Edward White, in making his decision to allow the government to take Indian land, rewrote history, arguing as he did that Congress had always had complete political power over Indian tribes.*

In the March 29, 1902, edition of *The Outlook* magazine, an article appeared entitled "Have Reservation-Indians Any Vested Rights?" Its author was George Kennan, *The Outlook's*

David Eugene Wilkins, *American Indian Sovereignty and the U.S. Supreme Court: The Masking of Justice*. Austin: University of Texas Press, 1997, pp. 64–117. Copyright © 1997 by the University of Texas Press. All rights reserved. Reproduced by permission of the University of Texas Press.

Washington correspondent. Kennan examined the federal government's policy of leasing tribal lands on the Standing Rock Sioux Reservation and concluded that Indian lands were not being protected, and were, in fact, being confiscated without tribal consent.

As evidence that this actually had happened, Kennan quoted from a decision rendered March 4, 1902, by the Court of Appeals of the District of Columbia in *Lone Wolf v. Hitchcock*. In this case, the court had held that the pertinent provisions of the 1868 treaty between the Kiowa, Comanche, and the United States did not give the tribes legally enforceable title to their lands. In the appeal judge's own amazing and prophetic words:

> The treaty of 1868 certainly did not vest in the Indians, either in their individual or tribal capacity, anything more than the right to occupy the lands as against the United States until it was found necessary to make other provisions for them. There was no grant of estates either of freehold or a leasehold; only a mere right to occupy and use the lands, according to the habits and customs of the Indians; but those rights of the Indians were sacred to them as against every one, until Congress made provision for assuming control over the lands, and making other disposition thereof, upon such terms and conditions as Congress should prescribe.

The issue of Congress's power to abrogate foreign and Indian treaties had been dealt with by the federal courts in several earlier cases. Those decisions, at least the ones involving Indian treaties, however, are clearly differentiated from *Lone Wolf* because they did not specifically involve a deprivation of tribal property rights previously acknowledged under a ratified treaty.

Historical Background

On October 21, 1867, representatives of the Kiowa and Comanche tribes (the Apache Tribe joined by separate treaty later) entered into a treaty with the seven-member delegation of the congressionally created Indian Peace Commission at Medicine Lodge Creek in Kansas. This multipurpose treaty entailed land cessions, the establishment of peace, and the creation of reservation boundaries. Moreover, it contained several "civilization" provisions, including the following: Indian parents agreed to send their children to schools; heads of households could select up to 320 acres for farming; and the Indians agreed to remain within boundaries of their newly established homelands.

The most relevant provisions, however, are found in articles 2 and 12 which deal with the establishment and protection of the three-million-acre reservation. . . .

Notwithstanding these legal and moral assurances, the fervor to individualize tribal land holdings following the passage of the 1887 General Allotment Act soon reached the confederated Kiowa, Comanche, and Apache (KCA) reservation.

In 1892, the three-member federal Cherokee Commission (also known as the Jerome Commission), established by Congress in 1889 to engage certain Oklahoma tribes in land cession agreements, concluded a pact with representatives from the KCA tribes for the allotment of their lands. The remaining "surplus" lands were to be opened for non-Indian settlement. Although a number of Indian signatures were obtained, the three-fourths requirement was not met. Nevertheless, the agreement was sent to Washington, D.C., for congressional ratification.

On October 20, 1893, 323 KCA tribal members memorialized the Senate, strenuously arguing that the October 6, 1892, agreement should not be ratified for several reasons. First, they stated that negotiating sessions had not, as required by law, been conducted "in open council nor in the presence or with the knowledge of their people [tribal leaders] and constituents. Second, they stressed that the commission, after having fraudulently obtained an inadequate number of signatures, then "caused numerous pretended councils of said Indians to be held under the guns of said fort" (Fort Sill), where additional—though still too few—signatures were gathered "by misrepresentation, threats, and fraud. . . ." Finally, that the government's commission then relocated to the Indian agency headquarters of Anadarko where, for "more than a month . . . it continued its campaign of mendacity, fraud, and coercion until the alleged signatures of 456 Indians were claimed to have been obtained." The tribal memorialists then asserted that once the 456 signatures had been collected, the "said agreement was, without the loss of an hour, but upon the same day, transmitted to Washington. . . ."

Despite the haste with which the agreement was shuttled to the Capitol, the ratification process would not be so quick. In 1898, five years from the date of the agreement's arrival in Washington, and after several previous attempts, a bill was finally reported out of committee on the House side favoring enactment of the 1892 agreement. This bill, however, substantially altered the original agreement by inserting a provision to hasten the settlement of Choctaw and Chickasaw claims to the Leased District. The KCA tribes had fought every legislative attempt to approve the agreement; nevertheless, the House bill was passed on May 16, 1898.

The Senate, however, bowing to pressure from the KCA tribes and a prestigious and influential interest group, The Indian Rights Association, adopted a resolution in January 1899 which directed the secretary of the interior to inquire whether the requisite number of signatures had been obtained. When Secretary Hitchcock responded on January 13, 1900, his startling findings confirmed the major contentions of the KCA tribes and their supporters. Hitchcock acknowledged that not only had "less than three-fourths of the adult males . . . signed" the agreement, but that the agricultural acreage provided for in the 1892 agreement was inadequate to meet the needs of the Indians.

W.A. Jones, the commissioner of Indian affairs, submitted equally revealing findings. The commissioner gave three reasons why he felt the agreement should not be ratified: (1) he questioned "when, if ever, the Indians [would] receive any compensation for their lands"; (2) he stated that "if the lands are paid for there is no certainty that the Comanche, etc., Indians will ever receive one cent"; and (3) he complained that the agreement, as amended, "made no provision for the payment of the interest to the tribes." The commissioner ended his remarks by suggesting that "the agreement should be rejected by Congress, or that it be ratified with the proposed amendments and submitted to the Indians for their acceptance or rejection." After all, noted Commissioner Jones, "it is certainly a novel proposition in law that one party to an agreement may, without the consent of the other, alter or modify an essential part of such contract." He concluded with, as it turned out, unwarranted faith in the legal system, that "no court of law would uphold or enforce any contract so altered or amended."

However sound these and the KCA tribes' arguments were, it was obvious that certain members of Congress intended to ratify the agreement over the considered opposition of the tribes and the Indian Affairs commissioner.

On June 6, 1900, nearly eight years after the original agreement was signed, the Senate passed the amended agreement without debate at the end of the session. Nothing in the title of the act indicated that section 6 was a ratification of the contested Jerome Agreement of 1892. Three supplementary acts enacted in 1901 expanded the manner in which ceded tribal lands were to be handled.

The Judicial Process Begins

Lone Wolf, a well-known Kiowa headman, supported by the Indian Rights Association, filed suit in the Supreme Court of the District of Columbia on June 6, 1901, to obtain an injunction to prevent implementation of the acts confirming the 1892 agreement. Lone Wolf and his associates lost in the District Court. They then appealed to the district court of appeals. Even as this appeal was pending, President [William] McKinley issued a proclamation on July 4, 1901, which said that the KCA-ceded surplus lands were to be opened for settlement from August 6, 1901.

The court of appeals also ruled for the United States. The court stated that reservation Indians with "assigned lands" had no vested rights but only a right to occupy "at the will of the government." The judges, however, after having savaged tribal treaty and property rights, ironically ended their opinion by piously intoning, "We shall be greatly gratified if that high tribunal [U.S. Supreme Court] may be able to find a way for affording a remedy for what is alleged to be a grievous wrong to the Indians."

Lone Wolf, also known as A. Kei-quodle, was joined by Eshitie, principal chief of the Comanche; White Buffalo, Ko-Koy-Taudle, Marmo-sook-car-we, Narwats, Too-wi-car-ne, William Tivis, and Delos K. Lone Wolf (Lone Wolf's interpreter). They were represented by William Springer and Hampton L. Carson. Ethan A. Hitchcock was joined by William A. Jones, commissioner of Indian affairs, and Binger Herman, commissioner of the general land office, as appellants.

Springer and Carson, on behalf of the KCA tribes, raised a number of compelling treaty and constitutional arguments in their brief before the Supreme Court that stress the importance of this case. First, they argued that the Court of Appeals had made a "fundamental error" in stating that Indians "had always been treated as wards with assigned lands and no defensible title." They noted that this was a "historical error and ignore[d] the feature of Indian consent."

Second, they cited the precedent established in *Mitchel v. United States* (1835) and reaffirmed in *Holden v. Joy* (1872) that Indian title was as "sacred as the fee-simple title of whites." And they brought forth another principle established in *Holden*—that Congress has no power to interfere with treaty rights, "except in cases purely political."

Third, they argued that the 1867 Medicine Lodge treaty was a binding contract. They said that agreements executed and confirmed by which the tribes "in consideration of the relinquishment of the right to use and occupy other lands," were binding upon both parties and could not "be annulled or abrogated without the consent of both parties."

Fourth, the tribes' attorneys maintained that the central issues in the case were not "political questions" and reminded the justices that the court of appeals itself had concluded its decision by stating that it hoped the Supreme Court would find a remedy for the Indians.

Fifth, the attorneys stated that tribal objections to the original amendment and Congress's unilateral amendments to the treaty, which were not submitted to the Indians for approval, portrayed a situation which "shocks the conscience of every person who believes in justice and fair dealing."

Sixth, Springer and Carson argued that the Indians had a vested right to their property and that under existing law legislative acts impairing such rights were void. They then cited *Marbury v. Madison*, and argued that since the essence of civil liberty was the right of every individual to have the protection of the law when an injury was sustained, the Supreme Court had the authority to provide a forum for the determination of what constitutes vested rights.

Seventh, they asserted that the Indians had a perpetual right of occupancy, that they were entitled to due process of law, that Indians were "persons" under the Constitution, and that the tribes' property had not been taken for "public use." This action by the government, argued the attorneys, was without precedent. Prior to the act of June 6, 1900, Congress had "never passed an Act which deprived Indians of the right to the use and occupancy of lands secured to them by treaty, without their consent, except by due process of law."

Eighth, Springer and Carson rejected the government's contention that as "wards," Indians had few rights. Moreover, they astutely noted that even if the Court insisted on treating the Indians as wards, even wards could not be divested of their title to lands without some kind of hearing.

Finally, Springer and Carson gave Congress the benefit of the doubt and said "there is some doubt even as to whether Congress really intended to ratify the so-called Jerome Agreement. . . ." They noted that the KCA Agreement, which had never been ratified by the Indians, had been dovetailed with the tribally approved Fort Hall Agreement. And they expressed doubt that a majority of Congress knew what was transpiring: "The fact that it was being amended and ratified without submission to the Indians for ratification or rejection does not appear to have been called to the attention of either House of Congress. It is highly probable, therefore, that but few Senators or members understood the full import of the measure."

The United States attorneys, Assistant Attorney General Willis Van Devanter . . . reached for and relied on the entrenched rhetoric of Indian "wardship" and argued that as "wards" tribes were fully controlled and cared for by Congress. Van Devanter said:

> It was demonstrated that the Indian [by this period] was absolutely incapable of protecting himself in his new surroundings or of determining what was for his advantage. . . .
> [T]o afford the Indian that protection which the laws of humanity demanded should be given him, and to prevent as far as possible the evil consequences to both parties which would necessarily flow from the clash between civilization and savageism, it was necessary that the Government should intervene and assume complete control over the Indians.

Another telling quote from Van Devanter's brief indicates how deeply the guardianship-wardship theory had seeped into the consciousness of government lawyers and policymakers. "While sentimentality may characterize the exercise of absolute authority over the affairs of the Indians as an abrogation of power because of might, yet the exigencies of the situation demanded its assumption and results have justified it."

Finally, Van Devanter reiterated a classic Darwinian cultural argument—that the federal government had legitimate authority to force the Indians to emerge from their alleged "savage" state. The essential step in this "cultural evolution" was individual ownership of land. . . .

In the Records and Briefs file of the case are two heart-rending letters written by Lone Wolf to his attorney, William Springer. The first, written December 27, 1901, reveals a man who was defiantly opposed to the selling of tribal lands, and who remained optimistic that the federal political and legal systems would protect his people's property and treaty rights. Lone Wolf informed Springer that the Kiowa Nation had instructed him to inform the government that they would not accept any monetary settlement offered by the United States for tribal lands being squatted on by whites. "We believe," said Lone Wolf, "that while everything seems to be against us, we will succeed. There is [a] just God who rules the affairs of this government." By July 1902, Lone Wolf's tone was noticeably more depressed. In a letter to Springer signed by Lone Wolf and sixteen other Indians, one senses the severe level of frustration now experienced by the tribesmen regarding their inability to protect their lands from white encroachment, notwithstanding their seemingly invincible legal and moral arguments. "Good friend," wrote Lone Wolf, "we, the undersigned members of the Kiowa and Comanche tribes, wish to write to you concerning our affairs. We think we ought to have by rights the say so in some things, but the way things are running we have no rights whatever." Lone Wolf's fears were soon to be realized.

Masking Within the Decision: The Opinion

The fate of the KCA tribes now lay at the Supreme Court's doorstep. In the ensuing decision, however, their hopes and, by implication, those of all tribes with treaty-based rights and desirable lands, were crushed. The Court's unanimous opinion represented a perfect and deadly synthesis of the plenary power concept and the political question doctrine. The Court refused, citing the political question doctrine, to even consider the tribes' core argument of "fraudulent misrepresentation" by government officials. The justices also refused to consider the issue of the Senate's unilateral alteration of the 1892 agreements provisions. Additionally, the Court ignored the fact that the KCA were not in a relation of dependency when they negotiated their treaty with the U.S. in 1867.

The only question the Court considered was whether the Act of June 6, 1900, was constitutional. Despite Lone Wolf's treaty and constitutional arguments, Justice White accepted the "wardship" arguments of Van Devanter and said that the Indians' treaty-defined property rights had vested not in themselves but in the federal government. This "contention" of the Indians, said White, "in effect ignores the status of the contracting Indians and the relation of dependency they bore and continue to bear toward the government of the United States." White was retroactively bestowing wardship status on the tribes to make the abrogation of their treaty rights appear legal. He went on: "To uphold the claim would be to adjudge that the indirect operation of the treaty was to materially limit and qualify the controlling authority of Congress in respect to the care and protection of the Indians, and to deprive Congress, in a possible emergency, when the necessity might be urgent for a partition and disposal of the tribal lands, of all power to act, if the assent of the Indians could not be obtained."

Masks of Dependency, Security, and Christian Morality

On the status of tribal lands, White first cited prior language in which the Court had equated Indian title with fee-simple title, and then proceeded to set up a situation in which he was able to circumvent these decisions. He said, "In none of these cases was there involved a controversy between Indians and the government respecting the power of Congress to administer the property of the Indians." This is correct, as written. Prior to this date, Congress had historically acknowledged that it had no right to challenge treaty-recognized property rights which, despite what White said, did indeed vest in the retaining party. One of the cases cited by White, however, *Beecher v. Wetherby* (1877), had stated that the United States had a superior authority over Indians based on guardianship and that such authority "might be implied, even though opposed to the strict letter of a treaty with the Indians." This "abrogation by implication" argument was then meshed with another *Beecher* precedent: that the United States' actions regarding tribes would be governed "by such considerations of justice as would control a Christian people in their treatment of an ignorant and dependent race." Here we see Christian theology being used to rationalize violations of constitutionally recognized treaty rights.

Displaying a lucid and self-contradictory ability to rewrite history in a way that legitimized congressional power over tribes, Justice White asserted that "[p]lenary authority over the tribal relations of the Indians has been exercised by Congress from the beginning, and the power has always been deemed a political one, not subject to the control of the judicial department of the government." Both of these statements are judicial myths, without historical justification. Congress has not had plenary power over the tribes from the beginning; nor has the power always been determined to be political.

White apparently said Congress *always* had plenary authority not subject to judicial review because the Court was intent on legitimating the congressionally inspired and presidentially executed breakdown of communally held tribal lands which, the Court had determined, was essential before Euro-American civilization could be approximated by detribalized Indian individuals.

For White, . . . the 1871 treaty-ending law was pivotal. Until that year, "the policy was pursued of dealing with the Indian tribes by means of treaties, and, of course, a moral obligation rested upon Congress to act in good faith in performing the stipulations entered into on its behalf." White then cited *Ward* and *The Cherokee Tobacco* as support. He was asserting that after 1871 Congress could selectively decide whether it wanted to act in a morally responsible way by fulfilling the provisions of extant treaties. White then stated the most powerful lines of the decision:

> The power exists to abrogate the provisions of an Indian treaty, though presumably such power will be exercised only when circumstances arise which will not only justify the government in disregarding the stipulations of the treaty, but may demand, in the interest of the country and the Indians themselves, that it should do so. When, therefore, treaties were entered into between the United States and a tribe of Indians it was never doubted that the *power* to abrogate existed in Congress, and in a contingency such power might be availed of from considerations of governmental policy, particularly if consistent with perfect good faith towards the Indians. (emphasis original)

White does not define the "contingency" spoken of or what the considerations of "governmental policy might be," or how overt treaty abrogation can be consistent with "perfect good faith" toward Indians when the Indians consider it a direct exercise of bad faith and a contravention of their treaty rights. This is a prime example of the Court's use of legal masks to deny the humanity of the Indians and mask their own violations of the law. The judiciary, acting purely and deferentially as a legitimator of congressional policy, simply "presumed" that Congress had acted in good faith in dealing with the tribes because subsequent to the treaties' ratification it could find no historical or legal assurance that Congress had "in reality" acted in good faith.

Congress, said the Court, had not only unlimited but unreviewable authority over Indian tribes, their treaties, and their properties. White and the Court were acknowledging that even if Congress had violated the treaty, had violated the Constitution's Treaty Clause, and had violated the principles of consent, fairness, and justice, the judiciary would not look behind the actions of the legislative bodies.

White concluded by reiterating his presumption of good faith in Congress's right to exercise plenary authority to transform tribal communal lands to individual parcels—a transformation Indians could not resist by challenging the government's actions in Court. As in *The Cherokee Tobacco*, the Indians learned that to gain any measure of justice they would have to petition Congress, the very branch intent on destroying the basis of tribalism—tribal lands. . . .

In sum, *Lone Wolf* mangled tribal sovereignty. Congressional plenary power, unconstrained by the Constitution, was interwoven with the political question doctrine and judicial deference to the legislature to form an almost impregnable shield which ignored the fact that tribal interests and federal interests could be in fundamental conflict. Although the Supreme Court had asserted that Congress's action was for a public purpose, one could powerfully argue that this was not the case since the lands taken were sold to white homesteaders. The 1900 agreement, therefore, "probably would not have been constitutional had the property been held by non-Indian owners."

A month after the decision, Senator Orville Platt (R., Connecticut) requested that extra copies of the decision be printed as a Senate document because "there is a great demand for it." When the Senate could not agree on the number of copies to be printed—500 or 1,000—Senator Matthew Quey (R., Pennsylvania) stepped forward and insisted that 1,000 copies were needed. His justification: "I think we better make the number of additional copies 1,000. It is a very remarkable decision. It is the *Dred Scott* decision No. 2, except that in this case the victim is red instead of black. It practically inculcates the doctrine that the red man has no rights which the white man is bound to respect, and, that no treaty or contract made with him is binding. Is that not about it?"

The Court's Justification

As federal political, economic, and military power waxed in the late nineteenth century, with the corresponding waning of tribal power in these areas, there was a change, sometimes gradual, sometimes abrupt, in the way tribal sovereignty was conceptualized by the Supreme Court. In [researchers Russel] Barsh and [James] Henderson's words, [in *The Road: Indian Tribes and Political Liberty*] by the time of *Lone Wolf*, "[t]ribal domestic sovereignty had been surreptitiously transmogrified, from exclusive to residual, from presumptively inherent to presumptively delegated." The concept "guardianship/wardship" was a principal element in this legal transformation.

In [chief justice John] Marshall's *Cherokee Nation* (1831) decision, there was an illusion of tribal wardship; beginning with *Kagama* [*v. United States*] (1886) and continuing, albeit inconsistently, throughout the next several decades, wardship had become a delusion. Marshall used the analogy of "Indians as wards" in 1831 to justify or rationalize the federal government's self-imposed right or power to "protect" Indian tribes, both from states and foreign nations. He said that the relationship between tribes and the states "resemble[d] that of a ward to his guardian," and that tribes, "as domestic-dependent nations," were in a "state of pupilage." In the Court's legal consciousness, by the last two decades of the nineteenth century and into the first several decades of the twentieth century, tribes were, and according to *Lone Wolf*, "had always been," wards subject to the plenary authority of the federal government, despite ample invalidating evidence. Reified in the Court's consciousness, the justices employed masks like "wardship," "dependency," "savagery," "primitivism," "plenary power," "political question" in various ways to achieve whatever ends they deemed viable. And it was the Court, not the tribe, the individual, the states, or even Congress, which retained plenary discretion to decide the scope of Congress's powers, and the degree, if any, to which treaty tribal rights were to be protected.

"Considerations of 'justice,' the jurists claimed, would govern all dealings 'with backward races.'"

Lone Wolf Affirmed the Status of Colonized People as Subjects

Blue Clark

Blue Clark is an instructor of law at Oklahoma City University School of Law. In the following excerpt from his book-length study of Lone Wolf v. Hitchcock, *Clark provides a judicial impact analysis of the* Lone Wolf *ruling. In his decision in the case, Justice Edward White had held that Congress has absolute power over Native American property and may dispose of it at its discretion. His decision made it legal for Congress to appropriate more than 2 million acres of land awarded in an 1868 treaty to the Kiowa, Comanche, and Apache peoples. Clark explains the ramifications of this decision on the rest of the world at a time when the United States was expanding as a colonial power. The idea of the subject status of Native Americans and the view that as wards they could not have complete self-government carried over into policies and treatment of other nonwhite peoples inhabiting other U.S.-colonized areas of the world.*

Lone Wolf occurred just at the peak of American patriotic fervor over acquisition of new overseas territories from Spain as a result of the Spanish-American War. The decree

Blue Clark, *Lone Wolf v. Hitchcock: Treaty Rights and Indian Law at the End of the Nineteenth Century*. Lincoln: University of Nebraska Press, 1996. Copyright © 1994 by the University of Nebraska Press. All rights reserved. Reproduced by permission of the University of Nebraska Press.

summarized America's approach to island peoples acquired in the takeover of Spanish colonial possessions after 1898. The subject status of the ward in *Lone Wolf* became the colonial status of the overseas dependent of the Insular Cases just at the time Uncle Sam "found new wards appealing to him for protection" during the same period, when the United States reached across the ocean for additional territory and subjects in the aftermath of the Spanish-American War. Humanitarians concerned with overseas natives in 1904 changed the title of the Friends of the Indian organization to the Lake Mohonk Conference of Friends of the Indian and Other Dependent Peoples. The latter name signified their enlarged interest a year after the *Lone Wolf* decision as a result of the wartime extension of United States authority. A process of colonial political incorporation and land expropriation on ocean possessions such as the Hawaiian Islands similar to the American Indian experience rapidly took place, leaving the native populace subordinate and increasingly landless.

The Subjection of Colonial Peoples

Lone Wolf placed colonial peoples in clear subject condition. One editorial remarked favorably that America was "taking on so many more 'wards of the Government' in different parts of the world." Henry Cabot Lodge, during Senate debate on the legal foundations for American colonial governance, summarized imperialists' views when he stated that national Supreme Court decisions declared "the United States could have under its control . . . a 'domestic dependent nation,'" thereby solving for all time in his mind "the question of our constitutional relations to the Philippines" and other territories. Guardianship over "dark skinned people" brought new obligations and stern responsibilities which called for severe policies. [Philippine rebel leader Emilio] Aguinaldo's claims to independent sovereignty and self-government in the Philippines were tolerated no more than were Lone Wolf's on the Kiowa Indian reserve.

Secretary of War Elihu Root, noted for forcing a thoroughgoing Army reorganization, commented that it would be as "preposterous" for Aguinaldo's men to exercise sovereignty over the Philippines as for Indians who aided the United States during the Indian wars to lay a claim of sovereignty over the vastness of America's Far West.

Judicial action, particularly the *Lone Wolf* case, also offered precedents. The decision itself reads like the summary of a patriotic Fourth of July oration, filled with rhetoric about "justice" by "a Christian people in their treatment of an ignorant and dependent race." The emphasis was on "the relation of dependency . . . towards the government of the United States," "the paramount power" that the legislative and judicial branches possessed over natives, as well as the untutored condition of peoples deemed by their very "weakness and helplessness" in questions of self-rule to require the guidance of a superior power. Secretary Root drew from Indian case law for legal assurance on the subject status of Filipinos. President [William] McKinley's instructions of April 7, 1900, to his Philippine Commission stressed that United States officials there "should adopt the same course" America used in dealing with Indians, permitting local limited tribal self-government that was carefully regulated and closely supervised. The United States did not recognize native governments in its new possessions, only American colonial regimes. Philippine Islands law officer Charles E. Magoon, in the Division of Insular Affairs, looked like the quintessential administrator. He was a corpulent attorney who was also an able overseas manager. He, too, quoted Supreme Court statements on Indians as guiding standards for Filipino rule.

In the Insular Cases, courts accepted expanded congressional power to control possessions just as the judiciary had done in the Kiowa case. American case law at the turn of the century set the legal stage for American overseas rule. American jurists drew a distinction between American Indian rulings and court decisions involving overseas possessions. In *Cariño v. the Insular Government of the Philippine Islands*, justices of the Supreme Court noted that domestic United States Indian policy was for the sole purpose of obtaining Indian lands, but that Philippine policy was in no way meant to exploit the Filipinos or their lands. The case of *Downes v. Bidwell* decided the question of American overseas rule under the United States Constitution. Territories abroad belonged to the United States, but their inhabitants possessed only the rights of natural law. They were not subject to Bill of Rights guarantees, a part of the ruling that quickly upset an advocate of black civil rights like John Marshall Harlan on the Court. Colonials' lives and commerce were "absolutely subject to the will of Congress." According to a dissenter on the High Court, Justice Edward Douglas White had argued in the majority opinion that Congress possessed the fullest power over the new territory "to keep it, like a disembodied shade, in an intermediate state of ambiguous existence for an indefinite period" of time.

Justice White championed the Insular Doctrine on the Supreme Court. His concept of "incorporated" and "unincorporated" territories in the cases comprised his most notable constitutional contribution to the law. As long as the newly acquired peoples were not citizens and none of the new territories were incorporated directly into the United States system, then Congress could dispose of the new territories more readily in the future. White made a distinction between areas annexed (unincorporated) and areas that were properly territory (incorporated). Citizenship and territorial status would not hamper congressional action. The new lands and their peoples were not under the Constitution's numerous restrictions dealing with new territories and citizenship. In chambers, it may have been Justice William Moody's lurid story graphically depicting the consequences of twelve tattooed savage chieftains filing into a jury room, resting their spears and war trophies against the wall, and deliberating evidence in a jury trial that swept the other justices along into supporting White's Insular Doctrine. The Doctrine provided a solution to the dilemma of how to deal with new peoples overseas without at the same time jeopardizing what they viewed as a precarious social and political balance at home.

Treatment of "Lesser" Peoples

Political leaders and legal scholars discussed the theoretical, moral, and practical problems of governing overseas possessions. Indian policy provided a domestic guide to overseas rule. The climate of opinion within the American nation regarding paternalistic treatment of "lesser" peoples created a popular acceptance of island possessions once American leaders determined that to be the proper national course of action. Some of the same rhetoric about guardian-ward relationships found its way into the debate regarding annexation of such insular areas as the Philippines. Even though it preceded the Kiowa case slightly, one magazine editorial argued in a similar vein of paternalistic obligation that United States soldiers in the Philippine archipelago were themselves faced with "the case of a child found upon a doorstep," since American troops were forced to govern a childlike tribal people. The national literary figure Mark Twain, known particularly for his humor, used stark anti-imperialist language in rebuttal to the editorial and pointed out that the United States "beguiled" Filipinos in the name of "civilization" in much the same fashion that government agents and missionaries had hoodwinked American Indians years before in a sleight of hand policy that had pledged great benefits to the Indians but in reality brought only misery and degradation.

Former president Theodore Roosevelt drew from his study and travels in western America for his observation that, like American Indians before them, Filipinos could only partake in self-government "under a wise supervision" that the United

States firmly administered over them. The United States could not turn its back on the national necessity of bringing order to chaotic tropical lands. America could not turn away from its overseas duty any more than it would be "incumbent upon us to leave the Apaches of Arizona to work out their own salvation, and to decline to interfere in a single Indian reservation" at home. Philippine Governor William Howard Taft informed his island audience at Union Reading College in late 1903 that since "civilization follows material development," it was clear that the Philippine Islands and other American possessions "needed the helping and guiding hand" of the Americans who knew how to instill "popular rule" after generations of experience as pioneers battling hostile forces. Indiana Senator Albert J. Beveridge impressed his audience with the observation that God "has made us [English-speaking peoples] adept in government that we may administer government among savage and senile peoples" in the Almighty's attempt to redeem the world. Moreover, another speaker assured listeners in upstate New York that dependent peoples did not automatically have the "capacity for self-government." It "is a result to be achieved by patient and persistent endeavor" on the part of those who were willing to make the sacrifice to show how to develop self-government.

Justice and Control

Imperialists resorted to the same smug phraseology the Supreme Court justices employed in their discussions of why the United States could seize Kiowa land. The High Court declared that the disposition of Indian lands would only be permitted when it was clearly "in the best interest of the Indians." Considerations of "justice," the jurists claimed, would govern all dealings "with backward races." It was America's mission "to establish . . . good government among less-favored nations." New subjects among island tribes would be treated like "tribal Indians" and as "wards" or "dependent nations." Advocates of national overseas dominion evoked nearly the same wording as the justices had used in the *Lone Wolf* decision when they talked about an overseas rule which "would be governed by such considerations of justice as would control a Christian people in their treatment of an ignorant and dependent race."

Indian Rights Association founder and leader Herbert Welsh turned much of his reform zeal toward anti-imperialism, devoting nearly all his energies after 1898 to opposing overseas dominion. He also drew his examples from Indian policy: "If upon the verge of a colonial policy we make stronger the precedent we have established of dealing with the Indians unjustly . . . so as to make vagrants and paupers of them, . . . our management of outside dependent peoples will be conducted in the same unhappy way," he wrote at the start of the nation's imperialistic adventure. Other anti-imperialists shared his views. One newspaper editorialized, "With the experience of the Indians . . . before us, is it not the height of folly for Americans to reach out after eight millions of aliens [overseas] . . . with mixed races, half-breeds, and blacks?" The paper asked, if Americans could not successfully rule other cultures at home, then how could the United States do so abroad in faraway places like the Philippines and Cuba? Still others raised questions about the unbridled power of Congress to deal with foreign nationals, a power that appeared to be "without any constitutional limits whatever." To them, imperialism raised unsettling questions of constitutional law. Ironically, imperialism involved for some writers more secure relations than had been operating for United States interaction with American Indians, because the new relationship would be based on the recent United States treaty with Spain concluding hostilities. They presumed American Indians no longer had any treaty relationship left.

CHAPTER 3

Compensating Indians for Illegal Seizure of Tribal Lands

Case Overview

United States v. Sioux Nation (1980)

In 1851, the United States signed the Treaty of Fort Laramie with the Lakota Sioux. That treaty promised 60 million acres of the *Paha Sapa*, or Black Hills, "for the absolute and undisturbed use and occupancy of the Sioux." White settlers of the time knew that the Black Hills were sacred to the Lakota, considered the womb of Mother Earth and the location of ceremonies, vision quests, and burials.

In 1857 Lakota leaders gathered to discuss the increasing number of white invaders in the Black Hills. As settlers continued to ignore the treaty boundaries and as the government began to build military posts to protect the white presence, a second Fort Laramie treaty was signed in 1868 reducing the Sioux land to 20 million acres. In 1874, the presence of gold was confirmed in the hills by General George Armstrong Custer and a group of geologists. A rush of miners invaded, and the government tried to coerce the Lakota into selling their remaining 20 million acres. When the Lakota refused, Congress enacted a new treaty in 1877, giving them control of the land. It was signed by only 10 percent of the adult male Lakota population. The Lakota never accepted the validity of the transaction and considered their land illegally seized by the federal government.

Beginning in the 1920s, the Sioux filed several suits to get back their stolen land. After Congress passed an act allowing the Sioux to submit claims before the Court of Claims, the Sioux specified that the government had seized the Black Hills illegally. This claim was dismissed in 1942, when the Court said it had no jurisdiction. In 1946, the Sioux resubmitted their claim to the Indian Claims Commission. In 1974, the Indian Claims Commission decided the Sioux were entitled to

$17.1 million for reimbursement and interest of 5 percent from the time the land was taken. That decision was affirmed in 1979 by the Court of Claims.

In 1980, the Supreme Court was called upon to review the Court of Claims' 1979 decision. On June 30, 1980, the Court decided the then-longest-running claim in U.S. history. In an 8-1 decision, the Supreme Court found that the government had taken the Black Hills from the Sioux without just compensation, in violation of the Fifth Amendment, and the Court awarded them more than $105 million—the original $17.1 million plus 103 years' worth of interest at 5 percent.

Writing for the majority, Justice Harry Blackmun rejected the idea that Congress had acted in good faith, and acknowledged that the underlying intention of the act was to assimilate the Sioux and to deprive them of their way of life. He said of the case, too, that "a more ripe and rank case of illegal dealings may never be found in our history." The sole dissenting voice, that of Justice William Rehnquist, argued that for the Sioux to claim compensation amounted to an effort at "revisionist" history, insisting that to grant the Sioux compensation would be to misunderstand the history of the settling of the American West, in which villainy was perpetrated by American Indians and whites alike. Blackmun dismissed Rehnquist's opinion as illogical, noting that no historians had been identified who held the position Rehnquist suggested regarding the cession of the Black Hills.

The Lakota Sioux have refused to accept the compensatory award, arguing that they cannot take money in exchange for sacred land. Further, accepting the money would legally terminate Sioux demands for return of the land. Since the case ended, the Lakota have occupied portions of the Black Hills, filed suit in federal courts against the government asking for the return of their land, and trying to secure passage of legislation to get their land back. So far, they have been unsuccessful. As of 2008, accruing compound interest on the settlement has brought the value of the claim to over $1 billion.

> *"An obligation on the part of the Government to make just compensation to the Sioux nation ... must now be paid."*

The Court's Decision: The Federal Government Unlawfully Seized the Black Hills from the Sioux

Harry Blackmun

Harry Blackmun, an associate justice of the Supreme Court from 1970 to 1994, is best known as the author of the majority opinion in the 1973 Roe v. Wade *decision, overturning laws restricting abortion. In the following opinion delivered in the case of* United States v. Sioux Nation, *Blackmun held that the United States must compensate the Sioux Nation more than a century later for seizing their land in violation of an 1868 treaty. Blackmun reviews the facts of the case, explaining that the Treaty of Fort Laramie had guaranteed the tribe ownership of the Black Hills, but in 1877 the government confiscated the land. He also surveys other cases of claims by Indians of violations of their property rights, including the Cherokee cases of the 1830s and* Lone Wolf v. Hitchcock *(1903). He explains that for years the Sioux sought court action to rectify the illegal seizure, and in 1979 the Court of Claims decided the Sioux were due $17.5 million for the market value of the land in 1877, along with 103 years worth of interest at 5 percent, for an additional $105 million. Justice Blackmun, in his decision, upholds the decision of*

Harry Blackmun, majority opinion, *United States v. Sioux Nation of Indians*, 448 U.S. 371 (1980).

the Court of Claims, recognizing the taking of a piece of property without just compensation and discrediting the presumption of congressional good faith set forth in Lone Wolf v. Hitchcock.

This case concerns the Black Hills of South Dakota, the Great Sioux Reservation, and a colorful, and in many respects tragic, chapter in the history of the Nation's West. Although the litigation comes down to a claim of interest since 1877 on an award of over $17 million, it is necessary, in order to understand the controversy, to review at some length the chronology of the case and its factual setting.

Historical Background

For over a century now, the Sioux Nation has claimed that the United States unlawfully abrogated the Fort Laramie Treaty of April 29, 1868, 15 Stat. 635, in Art. II of which the United States pledged that the Great Sioux Reservation, including the Black Hills, would be "set apart for the absolute and undisturbed use and occupation of the Indians herein named." The Fort Laramie Treaty was concluded at the culmination of the Powder River War of 1866–1867, a series of military engagements in which the Sioux tribes, led by their great chief, Red Cloud, fought to protect the integrity of earlier-recognized treaty lands from the incursion of white settlers.

The Fort Laramie Treaty included several agreements central to the issues presented in this case. First, it established the Great Sioux Reservation, a tract of land bounded on the east by the Missouri River, on the south by the northern border of the State of Nebraska, on the north by the forty-sixth parallel of north latitude, and on the west by the one hundred and fourth meridian of west longitude, in addition to certain reservations already existing east of the Missouri. The United States "solemnly agree[d]" that no unauthorized persons "shall ever be permitted to pass over, settle upon, or reside in [this] territory." Ibid.

Second, the United States permitted members of the Sioux tribes to select lands within the reservation for cultivation. In order to assist the Sioux in becoming civilized farmers, the Government promised to provide them with the necessary services and materials, and with subsistence rations for four years.

Third, in exchange for the benefits conferred by the treaty, the Sioux agreed to relinquish their rights under the Treaty of September 17, 1851, to occupy territories outside the reservation, while reserving their "right to hunt on any lands north of North Platte [River], and on the Republican Fork of the Smoky Hill River, so long as the buffalo may range thereon in such numbers as to justify the chase." Ibid. The Indians also expressly agreed to withdraw all opposition to the building of railroads that did not pass over their reservation lands, not to engage in attacks on settlers, and to withdraw their opposition to the military posts and roads that had been established south of the North Platte River.

Fourth, Art. XII of the treaty provided:

> No treaty for the cession of any portion or part of the reservation herein described which may be held in common shall be of any validity or force as against the said Indians, unless executed and signed by at least three fourths of all the adult male Indians, occupying or interested in the same.

The years following the treaty brought relative peace to the Dakotas, an era of tranquility that was disturbed, however, by renewed speculation that the Black Hills, which were included in the Great Sioux Reservation, contained vast quantities of gold and silver. In 1874, the Army planned and undertook an exploratory expedition into the Hills, both for the purpose of establishing a military outpost from which to control those Sioux who had not accepted the terms of the Fort Laramie Treaty and for the purpose of investigating "the country about which dreamy stories have been told." D. Jackson, Custer's Gold 14 (1966) (quoting the 1874 annual report of

Lieutenant General Philip H. Sheridan, as Commander of the Military Division of the Missouri, to the Secretary of War). Lieutenant Colonel George Armstrong Custer led the expedition of close to 1,000 soldiers and teamsters, and a substantial number of military and civilian aides. Custer's journey began at Fort Abraham Lincoln on the Missouri River on July 2, 1874. By the end of that month they had reached the Black Hills, and by mid-August had confirmed the presence of gold fields in that region. The discovery of gold was widely reported in newspapers across the country. Custer's florid descriptions of the mineral and timber resources of the Black Hills, and the land's suitability for grazing and cultivation, also received wide circulation, and had the effect of creating an intense popular demand for the "opening" of the Hills for settlement. The only obstacle to "progress" was the Fort Laramie Treaty that reserved occupancy of the Hills to the Sioux.

Having promised the Sioux that the Black Hills were reserved to them, the United States Army was placed in the position of having to threaten military force, and occasionally to use it, to prevent prospectors and settlers from trespassing on lands reserved to the Indians. For example, in September 1874, General Sheridan sent instructions to Brigadier General Alfred H. Terry, Commander of the Department of Dakota, at Saint Paul, directing him to use force to prevent companies of prospectors from trespassing on the Sioux Reservation. At the same time, Sheridan let it be known that he would "give a cordial support to the settlement of the Black Hills," should Congress decide to "open up the country for settlement, by extinguishing the treaty rights of the Indians." Sheridan's instructions were published in local newspapers.

Eventually, however, the Executive Branch of the Government decided to abandon the Nation's treaty obligation to preserve the integrity of the Sioux territory. In a letter dated November 9, 1875, to Terry, Sheridan reported that he had met with President [Ulysses S.] Grant, the Secretary of the Interior, and the Secretary of War, and that the President had decided that the military should make no further resistance to the occupation of the Black Hills by miners, "it being his belief that such resistance only increased their desire and complicated the troubles." These orders were to be enforced "quietly," ibid., and the President's decision was to remain "confidential."

With the Army's withdrawal from its role as enforcer of the Fort Laramie Treaty, the influx of settlers into the Black Hills increased. The Government concluded that the only practical course was to secure to the citizens of the United States the right to mine the Black Hills for gold. Toward that end, the Secretary of the Interior, in the spring of 1875, appointed a commission to negotiate with the Sioux. The commission was headed by William B. Allison. The tribal leaders of the Sioux were aware of the mineral value of the Black Hills, and refused to sell the land for a price less than $70 million. The commission offered the Indians an annual rental of $400,000, or payment of $6 million for absolute relinquishment of the Black Hills. The negotiations broke down.

In the winter of 1875–1876, many of the Sioux were hunting in the unceded territory north of the North Platte River, reserved to them for that purpose in the Fort Laramie Treaty. On December 6, 1875, for reasons that are not entirely clear, the Commissioner of Indian Affairs sent instructions to the Indian agents on the reservation to notify those hunters that if they did not return to the reservation agencies by January 31, 1876, they would be treated as "hostiles." Given the severity of the winter, compliance with these instructions was impossible. On February 1, the Secretary of the Interior nonetheless relinquished jurisdiction over all hostile Sioux, including those Indians exercising their treaty-protected hunting rights, to the War Department. The Army's campaign against the "hostiles" led to Sitting Bull's notable victory over Custer's forces at the battle of the Little Big Horn on June 25. That victory, of course, was short-lived, and those Indians who surrendered to the Army were returned to the reservation, and deprived of their weapons and horses, leaving them completely dependent for survival on rations provided them by the Government.

In the meantime, Congress was becoming increasingly dissatisfied with the failure of the Sioux living on the reservation to become self-sufficient. The Sioux' entitlement to subsistence rations under the terms of the Fort Laramie Treaty had expired in 1872. Nonetheless, in each of the two following years, over $1 million was appropriated for feeding the Sioux. In August 1876, Congress enacted an appropriations bill providing that "hereafter there shall be no appropriation made for the subsistence" of the Sioux, unless they first relinquished their rights to the hunting grounds outside the reservation, ceded the Black Hills to the United States, and reached some accommodation with the Government that would be calculated to enable them to become self-supporting. Act of Aug. 15, 1876, 19 Stat. 176, 192. Toward this end, Congress requested the President to appoint another commission to negotiate with the Sioux for the cession of the Black Hills.

This commission, headed by George Manypenny, arrived in the Sioux country in early September and commenced meetings with the head men of the various tribes. The members of the commission impressed upon the Indians that the United States no longer had any obligation to provide them with subsistence rations. The commissioners brought with them the text of a treaty that had been prepared in advance. The principal provisions of this treaty were that the Sioux would relinquish their rights to the Black Hills and other lands west of the one hundred and third meridian, and their rights to hunt in the unceded territories to the north, in exchange for subsistence rations for as long as they would be needed to ensure the Sioux' survival. In setting out to obtain the tribes' agreement to this treaty, the commission ignored the stipulation of the Fort Laramie Treaty that any cession of the lands contained within the Great Sioux Reservation would have to be joined in by three-fourths of the adult males. Instead, the treaty was presented just to Sioux chiefs and their leading men. It was signed by only 10% of the adult male Sioux population.

Congress resolved the impasse by enacting the 1876 "agreement" into law as the Act of Feb. 28, 1877 (1877 Act). 19 Stat. 254. The Act had the effect of abrogating the earlier Fort Laramie Treaty, and of implementing the terms of the Manypenny Commission's "agreement" with the Sioux leaders.

The passage of the 1877 Act legitimized the settlers' invasion of the Black Hills, but throughout the years it has been regarded by the Sioux as a breach of this Nation's solemn obligation to reserve the Hills in perpetuity for occupation by the Indians. One historian of the Sioux Nation [F. Fiske] commented on Indian reaction to the Act in the following words:

> The Sioux thus affected have not gotten over talking about that treaty yet and during the last few years they have maintained an organization called the Black Hills Treaty Association, which holds meetings each year at the various agencies for the purpose of studying the treaty with the intention of presenting a claim against the government for additional reimbursements for the territory ceded under it. Some think that Uncle Sam owes them about $9,000,000 on the deal, but it will probably be a hard matter to prove it.

Fiske's words were to prove prophetic.

The Court of Claims 1946–1979

Prior to 1946, Congress had not enacted any mechanism of general applicability by which Indian tribes could litigate treaty claims against the United States. The Sioux, however, after years of lobbying, succeeded in obtaining from Congress the passage of a special jurisdictional Act which provided them a forum for adjudication of all claims against the United

States "under any treaties, agreements, or laws of Congress, or for the misappropriation of any of the funds or lands of said tribe or band or bands thereof." Pursuant to this statute, the Sioux, in 1923, filed a petition with the Court of Claims alleging that the Government had taken the Black Hills without just compensation, in violation of the Fifth Amendment. This claim was dismissed by that court in 1942. In a lengthy and unanimous opinion, the court concluded that it was not authorized by the Act of June 3, 1920, to question whether the compensation afforded the Sioux by Congress in 1877 was an adequate price for the Black Hills, and that the Sioux' claim in this regard was a moral claim not protected by the Just Compensation Clause.

In 1946, Congress passed the Indian Claims Commission Act, creating a new forum to hear and determine all tribal grievances that had arisen previously. In 1950, counsel for the Sioux resubmitted the Black Hills claim to the Indian Claims Commission. The Commission initially ruled that the Sioux had failed to prove their case. The Sioux filed a motion with the Court of Claims to vacate its judgment of affirmance, alleging that the Commission's decision had been based on a record that was inadequate, due to the failings of the Sioux' former counsel. This motion was granted and the Court of Claims directed the Commission to consider whether the case should be reopened for the presentation of additional evidence. On November 19, 1958, the Commission entered an order reopening the case and announcing that it would reconsider its prior judgment on the merits of the Sioux claim.

Following the Sioux' filing of an amended petition, claiming again that the 1877 Act constituted a taking of the Black Hills for which just compensation had not been paid, there ensued a lengthy period of procedural sparring between the Indians and the Government. Finally, in October 1968, the Commission set down three questions for briefing and determination: (1) What land and rights did the United States acquire from the Sioux by the 1877 Act? (2) What, if any, consideration was given for that land and those rights? And (3) if there was no consideration for the Government's acquisition of the land and rights under the 1877 Act, was there any payment for such acquisition?

Six years later, by a 4-to-1 vote, the Commission reached a preliminary decision on these questions. *Sioux Nation v. United States*, 33 Ind. Cl. Comm'n 151 (1974). The Commission first held that the 1942 Court of Claims decision did not bar the Sioux' Fifth Amendment taking claim through application of the doctrine of res judicata [a "judged matter"]. The Commission concluded that the Court of Claims had dismissed the earlier suit for lack of jurisdiction, and that it had not determined the merits of the Black Hills claim. The Commission then went on to find that Congress, in 1877, had made no effort to give the Sioux full value for the ceded reservation lands. The only new obligation assumed by the Government in exchange for the Black Hills was its promise to provide the Sioux with subsistence rations, an obligation that was subject to several limiting conditions.... Under these circumstances, the Commission concluded that the consideration given the Indians in the 1877 Act had no relationship to the value of the property acquired. Moreover, there was no indication in the record that Congress ever attempted to relate the value of the rations to the value of the Black Hills. Applying the principles announced by the Court of Claims in *Three Tribes of Fort Berthold Reservation v. United States*, the Commission concluded that Congress had acted pursuant to its power of eminent domain when it passed the 1877 Act, rather than as a trustee for the Sioux, and that the Government must pay the Indians just compensation for the taking of the Black Hills.

The Government filed an appeal with the Court of Claims from the Commission's interlocutory order, arguing alternatively that the Sioux' Fifth Amendment claim should have been barred by principles of res judicata and collateral estoppel, or that the 1877 Act did not effect a taking of the Black Hills for which just compensation was due. Without reaching the merits, the Court of Claims held that the Black Hills claim was barred by the res judicata effect of its 1942 decision. The court's majority recognized that the practical impact of the question presented was limited to a determination of whether or not an award of interest would be available to the Indians. This followed from the Government's failure to appeal the Commission's holding that it had acquired the Black Hills through a course of unfair and dishonorable dealing for which the Sioux were entitled to damages, without interest, under 2 of the Indian Claims Commission Act. Only if the acquisition of the Black Hills amounted to an unconstitutional taking would the Sioux be entitled to interest.

The court affirmed the Commission's holding that a want of fair and honorable dealings in this case was evidenced, and held that the Sioux thus would be entitled to an award of at least $7.5 million for the lands surrendered and for the gold taken by trespassing prospectors prior to passage of the 1877 Act. The court also remarked upon President Grant's duplicity in breaching the Government's treaty obligation to keep trespassers out of the Black Hills, and the pattern of duress practiced by the Government on the starving Sioux to get them to agree to the sale of the Black Hills. The court concluded: "A more ripe and rank case of dishonorable dealings will never, in all probability, be found in our history, which is not, taken as a whole, the disgrace it now pleases some persons to believe."

Nonetheless, the court held that the merits of the Sioux' taking claim had been reached in 1942, and whether resolved "rightly or wrongly," the claim was now barred by res judicata. The court observed that interest could not be awarded the Sioux on judgments obtained pursuant to the Indian Claims Commission Act, and that, while Congress could correct this situation, the court could not. Ibid. The Sioux petitioned this Court for a writ of certiorari [review], but that petition was denied.

The case returned to the Indian Claims Commission, where the value of the rights-of-way obtained by the Government through the 1877 Act was determined to be $3,484, and where it was decided that the Government had made no payments to the Sioux that could be considered as offsets. App. 316. The Government then moved the Commission to enter a final award in favor of the Sioux in the amount of $17.5 million, . . . but the Commission deferred entry of final judgment in view of legislation then pending in Congress that dealt with the case.

On March 13, 1978, Congress passed a statute providing for Court of Claims review of the merits of the Indian Claims Commission's judgment that the 1877 Act effected a taking of the Black Hills, without regard to the defenses of res judicata and collateral estoppel. The statute authorized the Court of Claims to take new evidence in the case, and to conduct its review of the merits de novo [anew].

Acting pursuant to that statute, a majority of the Court of Claims, sitting en banc [as a body], in an opinion by Chief Judge Friedman, affirmed the Commission's holding that the 1877 Act effected a taking of the Black Hills and of rights-of-way across the reservation. In doing so, the court applied the test it had earlier articulated in *Fort Berthold*, asking whether Congress had made "a good faith effort to give the Indians the full value of the land," in order to decide whether the 1877 Act had effected a taking or whether it had been a noncompensable act of congressional guardianship over tribal property. The court characterized the Act as a taking, an exercise of Congress' power of eminent domain over Indian property. It distinguished broad statements seemingly leading to a contrary result in *Lone Wolf v. Hitchcock*, as inapplicable to a case involving a claim for just compensation.

The court thus held that the Sioux were entitled to an award of interest, at the annual rate of 5%, on the principal sum of $17.1 million, dating from 1877.

We granted the Government's petition for a writ of certiorari, in order to review the important constitutional questions presented by this case, questions not only of longstanding concern to the Sioux, but also of significant economic import to the Government.

Having twice denied petitions for certiorari in this litigation, we are confronted with it for a third time as a result of the amendment, above noted, to the Indian Claims Commission Act of 1946....

The Claim Is Upheld

The [evidence] ... fully support[s] the Court of Claims' conclusion that the 1877 Act appropriated the Black Hills "in circumstances which involved an implied undertaking by [the United States] to make just compensation to the tribe." *United States v. Creek Nation.* We make only two additional observations about this case. First, dating at least from the decision in *Cherokee Nation v. Southern Kansas R. Co.*, this Court has recognized that Indian lands, to which a tribe holds recognized title, "are held subject to the authority of the general government to take them for such objects as are germane to the execution of the powers granted to it; provided only that they are not taken without just compensation being made to the owner." In the same decision, the Court emphasized that the owner of such lands "is entitled to reasonable, certain and adequate provision for obtaining compensation before his occupancy is disturbed." The Court of Claims gave effect to this principle when it held that the Government's uncertain and indefinite obligation to provide the Sioux with rations until they became self-sufficient did not constitute adequate consideration for the Black Hills.

Second, it seems readily apparent to us that the obligation to provide rations to the Sioux was undertaken in order to ensure them a means of surviving their transition from the nomadic life of the hunt to the agrarian lifestyle Congress had chosen for them. Those who have studied the Government's reservation policy during this period of our Nation's history agree. It is important to recognize that the 1877 Act, in addition to removing the Black Hills from the Great Sioux Reservation, also ceded the Sioux' hunting rights in a vast tract of land extending beyond the boundaries of that reservation. . . . Under such circumstances, it is reasonable to conclude that Congress' undertaking of an obligation to provide rations for the Sioux was a quid pro quo [this for that] for depriving them of their chosen way of life, and was not intended to compensate them for the taking of the Black Hills.

In sum, we conclude that the legal analysis and factual findings of the Court of Claims fully support its conclusion that the terms of the 1877 Act did not effect "a mere change in the form of investment of Indian tribal property." Rather, the 1877 Act effected a taking of tribal property, property which had been set aside for the exclusive occupation of the Sioux by the Fort Laramie Treaty of 1868. That taking implied an obligation on the part of the Government to make just compensation to the Sioux Nation, and that obligation, including an award of interest, must now, at last, be paid.

The judgment of the Court of Claims is affirmed.

> *"Both settler and Indian are entitled to*
> *the benefit of the Biblical adjuration:*
> *'Judge not, that ye be not judged.'"*

Dissenting Opinion: Congress Did Not Act Unlawfully in Taking Sioux Land

William Rehnquist

William Rehnquist was nominated by President Richard Nixon to the Supreme Court, serving as an associate justice from 1972 to 1986 and holding the position of chief justice until his death in 2005. In his lone dissenting opinion in the case of United States v. Sioux Nation, *Rehnquist describes the attempt by the Sioux to claim compensation as an effort at "revisionist" history. He argues that the majority opinion in the case is based on an erroneous understanding of the settling of the American West. Referring to the "villainy" of the Sioux as well as the "greed, cupidity, and less-than-admirable" actions of the federal government, Rehnquist insists that it is not for the Court to assess history, and that both Indians and settlers are entitled to the biblical injunction "judge not, that ye be not judged."*

In 1942, the Sioux Tribe filed a petition for certiorari requesting this Court to review the Court of Claims' ruling that Congress had not unconstitutionally taken the Black Hills in 1877, but had merely exchanged the Black Hills for rations and grazing lands—an exchange Congress believed to be in the best interests of the Sioux and the Nation. This Court declined to review that judgment. Yet today the Court permits

William Rehnquist, *United States v. Sioux Nation of Indians*, 448 U.S. 371 (1980).

Congress to reopen that judgment which this Court rendered final upon denying certiorari in 1943, and proceeds to reject the 1942 Court of Claims' factual interpretation of the events in 1877. I am convinced that Congress may not constitutionally require the Court of Claims to reopen this proceeding, that there is no judicial principle justifying the decision to afford the respondents an additional opportunity to litigate the same claim, and that the Court of Claims' first interpretation of the events in 1877 was, by all accounts the more realistic one. I therefore dissent.

History of the Claim

In 1920, Congress enacted a special jurisdictional Act authorizing the Sioux Tribe to submit any legal or equitable claim against the United States to the Court of Claims. The Sioux filed suit claiming that the 1877 Act removing the Black Hills from the Sioux territory was an unconstitutional taking. In *Sioux Tribe v. United States* the Court of Claims considered the question fully and found that the United States had not taken the Black Hills from the Sioux within the meaning of the Fifth Amendment. It is important to highlight what that court found. It did not decide, as the Court today suggests, that it merely lacked jurisdiction over the claim presented by the Sioux. It found that under the circumstances presented in 1877, Congress attempted to improve the situation of the Sioux and the Nation by exchanging the Black Hills for 900,000 acres of grazing lands and rations for as long as they should be needed. The court found that although the Government attempted to keep white settlers and gold prospectors out of the Black Hills territory, these efforts were unsuccessful. The court concluded that this situation was such that the Government "believed serious conflicts would develop between the settlers and the Government, and between the settlers and the Indians." It was also apparent to Congress that the Indians were still "incapable of supporting themselves."

The court found that the Government therefore embarked upon a course designed to obtain the Indians' agreement to sell the Black Hills, and "endeavored in every way possible during 1875 and 1876 to arrive at a mutual agreement with the Indians for the sale. . . ." Negotiation having failed, Congress then turned to design terms for the acquisition of the Black Hills, which it found to be in the best interest of both the United States and the Sioux. The court found that, pursuant to the 1877 agreement, Congress provided the Indians with more than $43 million in rations as well as providing them with 900,000 acres of needed grazing lands. Thus, the court concluded that "the record shows that the action taken was pursuant to a policy which the Congress deemed to be for the interest of the Indians and just to both parties." The court emphasized:

> "[T]he Congress, in an act enacted because of the situation encountered and pursuant to a policy which in its wisdom it deemed to be in the interest and for the benefit and welfare of the . . . Sioux Tribe, as well as for the necessities of the Government, required the Indians to sell or surrender to the Government a portion of their land and hunting rights on other land in return for that which the Congress, in its judgment, deemed to be adequate consideration for what the Indians were required to give up, which consideration the Government was not otherwise under any legal obligation to pay."

This Court denied certiorari.

During the course of further litigation commencing in 1950, the Sioux again resubmitted their claim that the Black Hills were taken unconstitutionally. The Government pleaded res judicata [a matter already judged] as a defense. The Court of Claims held that res judicata barred relitigation of the question since the original Court of Claims decision had clearly held that the appropriation of the Black Hills was not a taking because Congress in "exercising its plenary power over

Indian tribes, took their land without their consent and substituted for it something conceived by Congress to be an equivalent." The court found no basis for relieving the Sioux from the bar of res judicata finding that the disability "is not lifted if a later court disagrees with a prior one." The court thus considered the equities entailed by the application of res judicata in this case and held that relitigation was unwarranted. Again, this Court denied certiorari.

Congress then passed another statute authorizing the Sioux to relitigate their taking claim in the Court of Claims. 92 Stat. 153. The statute provided that the Court of Claims "shall review on the merits" the Sioux claim that there was a taking and that the Court "shall determine that issue de novo [as a new case]." Neither party submitted additional evidence and the Court of Claims decided the case on the basis of the record generated in the 1942 case and before the Commission. On the basis of that same record, the Court of Claims has now determined that the facts establish that Congress did not act in the best interest of the Sioux, as the 1942 court found, but arbitrarily appropriated the Black Hills without affording just compensation. This Court now embraces this second, latter-day interpretation of the facts in 1877. . . .

Present Judgment Based on Revisionist History

Even if I could countenance the Court's decision to reach the merits of this case, I also think it has erred in rejecting the 1942 court's interpretation of the facts. That court rendered a very persuasive account of the congressional enactment. As the dissenting judges in the Court of Claims opinion under review pointedly stated: "The majority's view that the rations were not consideration for the Black Hills is untenable. What else was the money for?"

I think the Court today rejects that conclusion largely on the basis of a view of the settlement of the American West which is not universally shared. There were undoubtedly greed, cupidity, and other less-than-admirable tactics employed by the Government during the Black Hills episode in the settlement of the West, but the Indians did not lack their share of villainy either. It seems to me quite unfair to judge by the light of "revisionist" historians or the mores of another era actions that were taken under pressure of time more than a century ago. Different historians, not writing for the purpose of having their conclusions or observations inserted in the reports of congressional committees, have taken different positions than those expressed in some of the materials referred to in the Court's opinion. This is not unnatural, since history, no more than law, is not an exact (or for that matter an inexact) science.

But the inferences which the Court itself draws from the letter from General [Philip] Sheridan to General [William] Sherman reporting on a meeting between the former with President [Ulysses S.] Grant, the Secretary of the Interior, and the Secretary of War, as well as other passages in the Court's opinion, leave a stereotyped and one-sided impression both of the settlement regarding the Black Hills portion of the Great Sioux Reservation and of the gradual expansion of the National Government from the Proclamation Line of King George III in 1763 to the Pacific Ocean.

Ray Billington, a senior research associate at the Huntington Library in San Marino, Cal., since 1963, and a respected student of the settlement of the American West, emphasized in his introduction to the book *Soldier and Brave* (National Park Service, U.S. Dept. of the Interior, 1963) that the confrontations in the West were the product of a long history, not a conniving Presidential administration:

> Three centuries of bitter Indian warfare reached a tragic climax on the plains and mountains of America's Far West. Since the early seventeenth century, when Chief Opechancanough rallied his Powhatan tribesmen against the Virginia

intruders on their lands, each advance of the frontier had been met with stubborn resistance. At times this conflict flamed into open warfare: in King Phillips' rebellion against the Massachusetts Puritans, during the French and Indian Wars of the eighteenth century, in Chief Pontiac's assault on his new British overlords in 1763, in Chief Tecumseh's vain efforts to hold back the advancing pioneers of 1812, and in the Black Hawk War. . . .

. . . In three tragic decades, between 1860 and 1890, the Indians suffered the humiliating defeats that forced them to walk the white man's road toward civilization. Few conquered people in the history of mankind have paid so dearly for their defense of a way of life that the march of progress had outmoded.

This epic struggle left its landmarks behind, as monuments to the brave men, Indian and white, who fought and died that their manner of living might endure.

Another history highlights the cultural differences which made conflict and brutal warfare inevitable:

The Plains Indians seldom practiced agriculture or other primitive arts, but they were fine physical specimens; and in warfare, once they had learned the use of the rifle, [were] much more formidable than the Eastern tribes who had slowly yielded to the white man. Tribe warred with tribe, and a highly developed sign language was the only means of intertribal communication. The effective unit was the band or village of a few hundred souls, which might be seen in the course of its wanderings encamped by a watercourse with tipis erected; or pouring over the plain, women and children leading dogs and packhorses with their trailing travois, while gaily dressed braves loped ahead on horseback. They lived only for the day, recognized no rights of property, robbed or killed anyone if they thought they could get away with it, inflicted cruelty without a qualm, and endured torture without flinching.

That there was tragedy, deception, barbarity, and virtually every other vice known to man in the 300-year history of the expansion of the original 13 Colonies into a Nation which now embraces more than three million square miles and 50 States cannot be denied. But in a court opinion, as a historical and not a legal matter, both settler and Indian are entitled to the benefit of the Biblical adjuration: "Judge not, that ye be not judged."

"The Justice Department's case on appeals amounts to condoning retroactively [an] historical injustice."

Monetary Awards Cannot Compensate for Lost Tribal Land

Jill Norgren and Petra T. Shattuck

Jill Norgren is professor emeritus of government at John Jay College of Criminal Justice and the Graduate Center, City University of New York. The late Petra T. Shattuck was a legal scholar who specialized in the legal status of American Indians. In the following article, the authors comment on the case of the Justice Department in United States v. Sioux Nation, *in which the government was required to compensate the Sioux for illegally seizing the Black Hills in 1877. By appealing the case after it had been decided in favor of the Sioux decades ago and again in 1979, the United States seems to condone the historical injustice of the illegal seizure and reveal its disregard for tribal rights. Such an attitude smacks of imperialism, Norgren and Shattuck assert, and does not befit the commitment to human rights advocated by the administration of (then) president Jimmy Carter. That the administration regards returning sacred land as "too expensive" is another indication that native rights are not fully respected, the authors maintain.*

Jill Norgren and Petra T. Shattuck, "Black Hills Whitewash," *The Nation*, Vol. 230, May 10, 1980, pp. 557–560. Copyright © 1980 by The Nation Magazine/The Nation Company, Inc. Reproduced by permission.

In a decision [in 1979] that held the U.S. Government liable for the most "ripe and rank case of dishonorable dealing in our history," the United States Court of Claims awarded the Sioux Nation $103 million in damages. The court held that the U.S. Government's seizure by the Act of 1877 of 7.5 million acres of land in the Black Hills belonging to the Sioux Nation had violated the Fifth Amendment to the Constitution. The Sioux were awarded $103 million in damages—$17 million for the fair market value of the Black Hills in 1877, plus 5 percent interest on that amount compounded over 102 years. But the Justice Department appealed, and its arguments before the Supreme Court reflected attitudes toward Indians that were more appropriate to Gen. George Armstrong Custer's day than to our own.

It was Custer who in 1874 announced to the world that there was gold in the Black Hills and set off a clamor among white prospectors to take the land away from its Indian owners. The [Ulysses S.] Grant Administration, which had only six years earlier guaranteed the Sioux the "absolute and undisturbed use" of the land by solemn treaty, responded by first attempting to coerce the Indians to cede the Black Hills according to the 1868 treaty. When that failed, the Government forced the Sioux out. Federal agents disarmed the Indians, took away their ponies and "practically everything the Indians had" and, finally, threatened to cut off the Government rations on which the Indians were dependent. When a majority of the Indians still refused to turn over the Black Hills to the prospectors, Congress passed the Act of 1877, which accomplished the land-grab by fiat.

At the time, the U.S. Government justified its high-handed action by claiming that the Sioux were not self-sufficient. This contention was rich in irony since the 1868 treaty had already seized forty-eight million acres from the Sioux Nation, virtually eliminating its hunting ground, after the buffalo had been decimated by whites. When the Army dismounted and disarmed the Indians, they became totally dependent on the Government for food. In short, the U.S. Government took away the Indians' self-sufficiency, then pointed to their dependent state as proof of their inability to manage their own affairs.

Condoning Historical Injustice

The Justice Department's case on appeal amounts to condoning retroactively this historical injustice. Brushing aside the amply documented Court of Claims finding that the United States had "practiced duress on the starving Sioux" in expelling them from their land in order to open it up to gold prospectors, Deputy Solicitor General Louis Claiborne argued that the Government had been motivated solely by a concern for the best interests of the Sioux Nation. Turning history on its head, the Justice Department argued that no wrong had been done in 1877. It was as if the present West German Government were to defend the record of Nazi policies by claiming that [Adolf] Hitler's henchmen had, after all, believed their actions to be in the best interests of mankind.

The underlying premise of the Justice Department's brief is that conduct toward Indian tribes is exempt from the constraints of constitutional standards and international principles of human rights. In making that argument, the Justice Department did not hesitate to distort the historical record. It relied on court decisions of an era that paid scant attention to the rights of people who were not white and contended that Congress can break Indian treaties at will and exercise plenary, i.e., nearly absolute and unreviewable, power over Indians. The authority for this sweeping claim was the Supreme Court's 1903 decision in *Lone Wolf v. Hitchcock*. That the *Lone Wolf* case, which Judge Philip Nichols Jr. of the Court of Claims called "the Indians' Dred Scott decision [the 1857 case denying citizenship to blacks]," is still law is in itself an indictment of U.S. Indian policy. The Government's reliance today on a decision which, according to Judge Nichols, "certainly no Supreme Court past 1938 would make" shows that the Carter Administration's position in the Sioux case differs little from nineteenth-century views.

The Justice Department takes the position that Indian land has no constitutional protection and that the Government can, therefore, do virtually as it pleases with the property of Indians. What this means, says Steve Tullberg of the Indian Law Resource Center, is that "even land rights guaranteed by treaty are not worth the paper the treaty is written on." Or, as the Washington attorneys for the Sioux Nation put it, the Justice Department is urging the Supreme Court to amend the Fifth Amendment to make it read, "nor shall private property be taken for public use, without just compensation, *unless the property belongs to an Indian tribe.*"

In language that might make even a confirmed nineteenth-century imperialist blush, the Government's attorneys alleged that "the Indian tribes have been incapable of prudent management of their communal property" and that the United States must, therefore, do it for them. Moreover, "a disposal of tribal property in the discharge of this responsibility to manage the property for the tribe's benefit is an act on behalf of the tribe and, in effect, a disposal by the tribe." When the Government imposes its superior management ability on the incompetent tribe, the tribe must accept its actions for, as the Justice Department puts it, "a proper exercise of this power is no more a taking than would be a sale by the tribe itself." If, in its superior wisdom, the Government decides to alienate tribal land, it cannot possibly be accused of acting unconstitutionally because, in effect, the tribe itself sold the land. A more devastating combination of nineteenth-century racism with *1984* Orwellian double-think is difficult to imagine.

Jack Greenberg, director of the NAACP [National Association for the Advancement of Colored People] Legal Defense and Educational Fund Inc., terms the spectacle of such an argument being made in open court today without embarrassment "offensive in the extreme. It would be over the front page of every newspaper if it were made with respect to black or Hispanic people."

The Justice Department's cavalier disregard for the constitutional protections of tribal rights offends not only civil rights lawyers; it also comes as a shock to those who have applauded the Carter Administration's advocacy of human rights in world politics. Apparently the "abiding commitment [of the American people] to the full realization of human rights ideals" which Mr. Jimmy Carter pledged at the United Nations General Assembly only a few years ago does not apply to Native Americans. Given the occasion to right—in a very limited way—a historic wrong, the Carter Justice Department now argues that it is too expensive to do so, that the United States did no wrong in any case and that the American Indians are legally incompetent to judge their own best interests.

No Land for Dollars

Today, an increasing number of Indian nations are charging the United States Government with violating their social, economic and political rights. The refusal of the United States to return land illegally seized from Indians is considered the most glaring example of such infringements. For these Indians—the more tradition-minded members of the Lakota, Creek, Seminole, Iroquois Six Nations Confederacy, Hopi, Western Shoshone, Northern Cheyenne and Sioux tribes—the ultimate financial settlement in the case now before the Supreme Court is irrelevant, for it begs what to them is the real and far more profound question: return of the land and with it the possibility of preserving the Indian way of life. Land, the traditional Indians have said, is "our heritage, our homeland and our birthright," and it will not be sold "for a few pieces of silver."

Return of the land, is, however, an alternative that the Government is unwilling to consider. Since Congress created the Indian Claims Commission (I.C.C.) in 1946, the Government has used monetary compensation to absolve itself of responsibility for illegal and immoral seizure of Indian land. Not incidentally, such payments extinguish Indian title to the land.

It is exactly this unwanted trade of land for dollars that many Native Americans refuse to accept. Tradition-minded members of the Hopi tribe have long opposed monetary settlements for expropriated lands. In the late 1940s, the Bureau of Indian Affairs urged the Hopi to file a monetary claim with the I.C.C. for millions of acres. Much of this land was considered sacred land by the tribe—they called it "our Jerusalem." "We cannot and will not file any claims," the traditional Hopi wrote President [Harry] Truman. "This land is not for leasing or for sale. This is our sacred soil."

Shoshone leaders are equally adamant in their rejection of an award of $26 million by the I.C.C. as restitution for the Government's illegal seizure of twenty-four million acres in 1872. "We never lost that land, we never left it, and we're not selling it," they protest. "In our religion it's forbidden to take money for land. What's really happening is that the Government, through the Claims Commission, is stealing the land right now."

Although a large segment of the Sioux people have also demanded return of the Black Hills rather than accept monetary compensation for them, the tribe's Washington lawyers have not raised that issue. Their brief not only fails to demand a settlement that goes beyond money, it gratuitously concedes "the right of the Government in the exercise of its plenary power to extinguish Indian rights without any constitutional restraint and without judicial review." Only the amicus [friend of the court] brief filed by the Indian Law Resource Center focuses on the failure of Congress, the executive branch and the courts themselves to provide the same "unflinching constitutional protections to Indian interests [which they have] accorded all others." The second-class legal status imposed on Indians, the center argues, is "racist law" and denies Indian human rights.

If the Supreme Court rules in favor of the Sioux and awards the $103 million, a small step in the process of redressing the wrongs committed by the American Government will have been taken. Money payments alone, however, cannot satisfy fundamental human-rights principles. Such a decision would still apply a legal double standard to Indian land. Justice Hugo Black's admonition that "great nations, like great men, should keep their word," remains unheeded.

Since the Washington attorneys representing the Sioux do not speak for members of the tribe who want their land back, not money, they argue that "the concern of this case is with just compensation, not good or evil." But given America's legacy of brutality and racism toward Indians, the Government's arrogant challenge to the Court of Claims award in the Sioux case, if it prevails, would enshrine the evils of the past as official U.S. policy today.

> *"As for the Sioux, the claims process has encouraged them to evade any real responsibility for repairing the tragic condition of their lives."*

The Sioux Mismanaged the Black Hills Case

Edward Lazarus

Edward Lazarus, a lawyer, is the son of Arthur Lazarus Jr., one of the principal attorneys in the United States v. Sioux Nation. *In that case, the Supreme Court held that the United States should compensate the Sioux for illegally taking their land in violation of an 1877 treaty. While the Sioux refused the settlement of over $100 million in monetary compensation, insisting that they wanted no less than their land back, the white lawyers who defended the tribe earned in excess of $10 million. Lazarus defends the actions of his father, who has been vilified by many Sioux, and also claims that the tribe has not acted responsibly in regard to the case.*

On July 1, 1980, the day after the Supreme Court decision [in *United States v. Sioux Nation*], a former tribal council member from Pine Ridge, C. Hobart Keith, filed a complaint in the United States District Court for the District of Columbia, belatedly seeking an injunction to prohibit Arthur Lazarus "from pursuing a monetary award in the Black Hills case on behalf of the Oglala Sioux Tribe contrary to the desires and best interests of the Oglala Sioux people." Keith claimed that, because the Oglalas had permitted Lazarus's contract to expire, his representation of them was "illegal and contrary to law." Unless the court stopped Lazarus's representation, Keith further alleged, the Oglala Sioux would "lose the possibility of having their sacred lands in the Black Hills returned to them, since acceptance of the monetary award by the Oglala Sioux people fully discharges the United States of all claims and demands touching any matter involved in the Black Hills controversy."

On July 9, at a public meeting held at the Porcupine community on Pine Ridge, Oglala attorney Mario Gonzalez announced that he would ask the Supreme Court to declare a mistrial in the Black Hills claim on the ground that Lazarus had represented the Oglala Sioux without a valid contract. Gonzalez also declared his intention to seek an injunction barring the Secretary of the Interior from developing any plan to distribute the judgment money to the various Sioux tribes without their prior consent.

Two days later, on July 11, the Black Hills Sioux Nation Council reiterated its recent position repudiating monetary compensation for the Black Hills. "We've got a treaty and that's it," Reginald Bird Horse, a delegate from Standing Rock, told the press. "We are not going along with the sale of the land in the original boundaries of the 1868 Treaty." In the view of Simon Broken Leg, a Rosebud Sioux delegate, the Black Hills judgment would yield only $300 to each Sioux claimant (the actual amount would have been closer to $1,500 if the judgment were distributed per capita). After spending the money, Broken Leg asked, "then what you got tomorrow? You got no land; you got no future; you got no nothing."

At the time of the judgment, [the Indians' counsel Marvin] Sonosky had doubted that the land return movement would hold much sway in the elected tribal councils. He described the Sioux politicians who spurned the Black Hills judgment and demanded a land return as "a minute dissident group that is loud and articulate." Sonosky predicted that "the leaders of the tribal councils [would] accept the money."

But this was the view from Washington. Closer to the reservation, Vine Deloria, Jr., observed that "in the last five years so many people have moved to a hard-line position that any kind of solution that doesn't include land just won't be accepted. You'd be taking your life into your own hands if you went out on one of those reservations and preached just a cash settlement."

Deloria proved to be the better analyst. On July 9, having kept its silence until after the Supreme Court issued its decision, the Oglala Sioux tribal council unanimously adopted a resolution disavowing any participation in the Black Hills just compensation claim and declaring that the Supreme Court decision should be vacated "on the grounds that the Tribe was not represented by counsel in those proceedings." In addition, the Oglalas authorized Gonzalez to initiate new "legal proceedings . . . for trespass and a return of land. . . ."

In August, the Cheyenne River Sioux tribal council joined the Oglalas in repudiating the Black Hills award. "The welfare of ourselves and our descendants will not be promoted by accepting an award of money for our claim to the Black Hills of South Dakota," the council members unanimously resolved. "We hereby reject any award of money for the Black Hills . . . and do not abandon our claim to the lands taken by the Act of 1877."

Over time, all the Sioux tribal governments turned their backs on a court award of $106 million that everyone agreed was desperately needed for housing, food, health care, education, alcohol treatment, and a host of other basic necessities. Some Sioux leaders, like Cheyenne River Treasurer Mona Cudmore, regretted the decision. She wanted "to accept the settlement and get on with the business of planning some development and at least get some of the money for those of us who will use [it]." Any other choice, Cudmore thought, was simply unrealistic. "With the world situation being what it is today, it would be futile to think we would ever get the Black Hills back."

In the tribal councils, though, different priorities and different logic prevailed. At the council meetings and all over the reservations old traditionals and angry young Sioux, still partners in the revival of tribal traditions, successfully portrayed "acceptance" of the Black Hills award as a betrayal of everything Indian and everything Sioux. Invoking the treaty, invoking the belief that the Great Spirit had given the Black Hills to the Sioux as a permanent gift, passionate voices demanded that the councils fight for the land. "I cannot accept money for the Black Hills," Severt Young Bear, a young activist, explained, "because land is sacred to me. . . . [The whites] are trying to change our value system. To be a traditional person is to believe in our own culture, is to believe in yourself as a Lakota person; then you cannot sell the land."

Sioux leaders faced a choice that was really no choice at all. On the one hand, if they voted to use the Black Hills money, they faced certain accusation of having repudiated their heritage and having accepted as justly resolved the tribe's grievances against the United States that for a century had served to explain and excuse four generations of shattered lives.

On the other hand, if Sioux leaders voted to reject the Black Hills money, they could don the mantle of traditionalism (some sincerely, others not) while in fact sacrificing nothing. Regardless of what the tribal councils might say about "rejecting" the Supreme Court's just compensation award (which they also erroneously referred to as a "settlement"), after the Court's decision, the Black Hills judgment funds belonged irrevocably to the modern Sioux tribes. Even if the tribal councils never decided to use their $106 million, the money would remain in the Treasury invested on their behalf at interest rates varying between 8.75 and 10.25 percent. In other words, the tribal councils could always change their minds about using the money at no penalty.

By refusing to touch the Black Hills money, Sioux leaders also avoided the potentially disastrous results of distributing the judgment funds to their impoverished constituents. The eldest Sioux still remembered with bitterness and disappointment what happened after the last large cash infusion into Sioux country when Indian stockmen had sold their cattle herds during World War I. As Fools Crow recalled, the Sioux had "exchanged their freedom for money and liquor."

Vine Deloria, Jr., foresaw history repeating itself if the various Sioux tribes divided most of the Black Hills award into per capita payments. "With the distribution of funds," Deloria prophesied "will come the drug dealers, bootleggers, used car dealers, and appliance salesmen who would ordinarily cross the street to avoid saying hello to an Indian. One great spasm of spending will occupy [them] and then the people, as poor as they ever were, will return to normal lives."

Nor were most Sioux any more sanguine about what would happen if the tribal governments somehow resisted the pressure to distribute the Black Hills money per capita and, instead, channeled the award into new or existing tribal programs. For a dozen years the U.S. government had poured tens of millions of dollars into Sioux tribal governments and the people had little to show for it except their bare survival. Tribal leaders, common sentiment held, specialized mainly in nepotism, petty graft, and "business" trips. By dint of hard experience, the Sioux had grown almost boundlessly cynical about the ability of their tribal leaders to improve their lives. Many shared the view of Ramon Roubideaux that if the Black Hills money bypassed the liquor stores and used car salesmen, it would be "squandered by our bureaucratic tribal officials."

Given the widespread belief that the Black Hills award could be of no long-term benefit, the notion of holding out for a better deal—a return of the Black Hills themselves and perhaps a lot more money in damages—was enormously attractive, especially to a people ignorant of Washington and unable to assess independently their chances for success. Thus, amid much talk of sovereignty, sacredness, and ultimate triumph, the Sioux renewed the Black Hills fight, now more than a century old.

For sixty years, the direction and strategies for pursuing the Black Hills claim had emanated from white attorneys whom the Sioux had hired to navigate it through legal waters that they themselves could not fathom. But *that* Black Hills claims voyage was now safely over. The Indians could jettison their old pilots and follow their own hearts in setting new courses for their claim. The Sioux now had lawyers of their own to take the helm and attempt to steer the tribe through the perils of the white system. And Gonzalez stepped forward to take a turn at the wheel, a novice on a rough sea.

On July 18, Gonzalez filed suit against the United States asking for a return of the Black Hills lands and $11 billion in damages—$1 billion for "hunger, malnutrition, disease and death" and another $10 billion for the removal of nonrenewable resources from the Hills. Gonzalez based the Oglalas' complaint on his long-espoused legal theory that the United States seizure of the Black Hills violated the Fifth Amendment's requirement that governmental takings be for a "public" purpose and was, therefore, null and void. "We are arguing . . . that Congress cannot take Indian land and give it out to private homesteaders, mining interests, and other individuals," Gonzalez explained. "That is not a taking for public purposes." Accordingly, he argued, the Sioux had remained "the rightful owners [of the Black Hills] from 1877 to the present time."

Gonzalez believed that the $10 billion in damages for trespass and illegal use of the Black Hills was "quite conservative in view of the fortunes and property values claimed by the present illegal occupants of our Black Hills land." Gonzalez described the $1 billion for personal damages as a "pittance" compared to the suffering the Sioux had endured in the last century.

Like another lawyer who had represented the Sioux, Gonzalez assured his clients of success. "We feel our case has a lot of merit," he proclaimed. "We will win this case." And as the Sioux had placed their faith in [previous counsel] Ralph Case's extravagant promises, so the Oglalas trusted Gonzalez when he told them that under the white man's law, in the white man's courts, they could recover the Black Hills and a previously undreamed-of fortune, too.

After filing his land return suit, Gonzalez spent the balance of July and August seeking to prevent the Secretary of the Interior from actually paying out to the Oglalas any part of the $106 million Sioux judgment fund—thereby allegedly endangering the tribe's new lawsuit. On behalf of the Oglalas, Gonzalez also filed a Motion to Change Attorney with the Court of Claims, which had retained jurisdiction over the original Black Hills claim for the purpose of determining Sonosky and Lazarus's attorneys' fees. Charging Lazarus with "fraud of counsel" and "conduct which may conceivably result in an action for malpractice," Gonzalez told the court that "it is inappropriate for Mr. Lazarus to collect a fee for misconduct." Instead, Gonzalez argued, the court should oust Lazarus as the Oglalas' counsel.

Lazarus responded testily. "The case is over," he pointed out. "With the exception of applications for allowance of attorneys' fees . . . no further action remains to be taken in this litigation. The Tribe's request for permission to change attorneys, therefore, is moot." Lazarus also argued that the Oglalas' motion was inappropriate. "To allow a stranger at this late date in the proceedings to appear as attorney of record for any plaintiff would do a positive disservice to the lawyers involved and to the Court." If the Oglalas wished to contest his fee, Lazarus added, they would have ample opportunity to do so after his fee application was actually filed.

Although Lazarus seriously doubted that the Court of Claims would grant Gonzalez's motion, he nonetheless resented its contents as well as Gonzalez's frequent allegations in Sioux country, amplified in the press, that his handling of the Black Hills claim had been incompetent and deceitful. In response to Gonzalez's charges, Lazarus asked the trial judge in the still-pending 1868 treaty case to permit him to withdraw as counsel for the Oglalas. But the judge refused on the ground that his withdrawal would leave the tribe unrepresented. And although the judge invited the Oglalas to replace Lazarus, they did not do so, leaving him no choice but to continue to represent them even as they smeared his name.

Hobart Keith withdrew his lawsuit against Lazarus before any response was required. The Court of Claims rejected Gonzalez's motion to change attorneys.

The federal district court in Rapid City [South Dakota] also dismissed Gonzalez's land return and damages suit against the United States (*Oglala Sioux Tribe v. United States*). As Lazarus had predicted, the court ruled that it was without jurisdiction to consider the Oglalas' land return claim because the United States had not waived its sovereign immunity to such a suit. Gonzalez vowed to appeal.

On October 6, Lazarus filed a motion for attorneys' fees (for himself, Sonosky, and [attorney William Howard] Payne) in the Court of Claims, which, under the ICC [Indian Claims Commission] Act, had authority to award fees in any amount not exceeding 10 percent of the claims judgment. After a sixty-one page history of services rendered for the tribe, Lazarus argued that the maximum fee was more than justified. "From any perspective," he asserted in the necessarily immodest application, "the results we achieved in this case are nothing short of sensational. Viewed from the 1956 affirmance of the Commission's dismissal . . . the ultimate award of almost

$106 million borders on the miraculous. That accomplishment, unique and without precedent in the annals of American jurisprudence, fully justifies [the requested] fee. . . ."

[Indian leader] Russell Means filed an opposition to the fee application, repeating the familiar accusation that the attorneys had prosecuted a "claim for money without proper authorization and without the understanding and consent of the Dakota people. . . ." A group of old dealer traditional leaders from the Standing Rock Reservation (designating themselves the Yanktonai Bands of the Dakotah Nation, Inc.) expressed similar dissatisfaction with Sonosky and Lazarus's authorization. "IRA [Indian Rights Association] and modern day tribal council have hired these lawyers without involvement of the people," they complained. "[The attorneys'] claim must *not* be allowed in any amount."

Gonzalez did not oppose the fee application on behalf of the Oglalas, evidently believing that he had blocked payment to Lazarus through other channels. In *Oglala Sioux Tribe v. United States*, the Oglalas' land return suit, Gonzalez and the United States attorney had stipulated that no officer of the United States would "tender payment" of any part of the Black Hills award or take any other action to disturb the status quo between the parties pending the outcome of the tribe's appeal. Gonzalez interpreted the agreement as barring the United States from paying Lazarus attorneys' fees out of the Black Hills judgment fund. He was wrong.

On May 20, 1981, in a unanimous *en banc* [with the full court sitting] opinion, the Court of Claims awarded Lazarus, Sonosky, and Payne $10,595,943 in attorneys' fees, the maximum 10 percent. "The result the attorneys have obtained for their clients has been extraordinary," Chief Judge Friedman wrote in summary of the court's view.

> Starting with a case that appeared doomed, they obtained an award of more that $100 million—which is more than twice as large as any other made in an Indian claims case.

Both the attaining of any award and the magnitude of the award made were attributable solely to the endeavors of the attorneys. Considering all the circumstances—the nature of the case, the obstacles the attorneys had to overcome, the low initial prospect of success, and the great skill and dedication with which the attorneys did their work—we conclude that attorneys' fees of 10% of the award, or $10,595,943, are appropriate.

The fee decision, not surprisingly, made front-page news, as in the *New York Times*, which ran a long story and a photograph of Lazarus, Sonosky, and Payne under the banner headline "Big Wampum for a Legal Tribe." According to Stephen Glasser, publisher of the *Federal Attorneys' Fee Awards Reporter*, the $10.6 million Sioux fee ranked as one of the largest, if not the largest, fee ever awarded by a court.

The response in Sioux country was predictable. Having argued for years that Sonosky and Lazarus represented the Sioux solely out of financial self-interest, AIM [American Indian Movement] leader Russell Means denounced the lawyers as "parasites" and called the fee "the largest rip-off of Indian claims money in the history of this country." To Gonzalez the whole fee proceeding was a "sham." Other commentators concurred in the judgment of prize-winning author Peter Matthiessen, who wrote in his book *In the Spirit of Crazy Horse* (a Sioux history focused on the 1975 Pine Ridge murder of two FBI agents) that the Black Hills claim "had been won by the wealthy lawyer [Lazarus] and lost by his poverty-stricken clients. . . ."

Sonosky shrugged off the criticism, most of which (because of the Oglala contract expiration issue) was directed at Lazarus. In 1956, Sonosky had gambled that he could win the Black Hills claim and that gamble had paid off handsomely. The Court of Claims fee decision made Sonosky a rich man overnight. His personal share amounted to more than $4.8 million.

Like a grandfather recounting the hardships of his youth, Sonosky was fond of recalling the old days when he "had to support two practices, one to keep my family alive and the other to keep this [Black Hills] case going." Sonosky remembered working "terrible hours" researching the Black Hills claim, "then doing my paying oil, gas, and mineral cases on the side." He even went through the archives by himself, too poor to afford a researcher. Those days were now gone forever, of course, and Sonosky, over seventy, could easily have retired. But he loved his work and his image as a wily old Indian hand. He kept at his practice full-time at the small firm he had built over the years.

William Howard Payne, who had done no legal work on the Black Hills claim, received a fee of almost $700,000. Richard Case, Ralph Case's son and a successful Baltimore attorney, also received $25,000 pursuant to an old agreement that Sonosky had negotiated to settle his father's interest in the case.

The remaining $5 million belonged to Lazarus's firm, which rewarded him with a one-time year-end bonus of $150,000. From Sonosky, Lazarus also received a case of very expensive champagne. In July, as the now unrelenting attacks on his professional conduct reached a crescendo, after a year of heavy traveling and insufficient attention to diet, he entered a hospital suffering from a bleeding ulcer.

Shortly after the fee award, the United States Court of Appeals for the Eighth Circuit (the federal appellate court for South Dakota) affirmed the dismissal of the Oglalas' land return and damages action against the United States. Echoing the district court, the Eighth Circuit ruled that "Congress has deprived the district court of subject matter jurisdiction by expressly providing an exclusive remedy for the alleged wrongful taking [of the Black Hills] through the enactment of the Indian Claims Commission Act." Gonzalez promised to take the Oglalas' case to the Supreme Court and did so, fruitlessly. In January 1982, the Court declined to review the Eighth Circuit's decision.

Even before Gonzalez's latest setback, the Dakota chapter of AIM had grown impatient and disillusioned with the prospect of achieving a return of the Black Hills through the judicial process. "If Indian people think we can get the Black Hills back only by going to Court, then we must not remember our history," observed Bill Means, Russell's brother and the head of Dakota AIM.

On April 4, 1981, an AIM caravan of twenty cars left the Porcupine community on Pine Ridge, entered the Black Hills, and established a camp in Victoria Creek Canyon, a well-watered site surrounded by lush ponderosa pine about a dozen miles southwest of Rapid City. Dakota AIM justified the Black Hills occupation as the Indians' legal right under the 1868 treaty, the American Indian Freedom of Religion Act of 1978, and a federal statute dating to 1897 that permitted the use of wilderness sites for educational and religious purposes. AIM named the camp after Raymond Yellow Thunder, the Sioux from Porcupine whom the Hare brothers had killed in Gordon, Nebraska in 1972.

By noon, the Indian occupiers had started building tipis and settling in. Chief Frank Fools Crow came to bless the camp the next day. "Remain strong in your commitment," he told the Indians, "and you will win." Ron Two Bulls, a security guard at Yellow Thunder, took Fools Crow's words to heart. "I've been waiting for this for many years," he said of the occupation. "There's going to be a lot of us that will probably die here."

Despite the "last stand" rhetoric, no one perished at Yellow Thunder. And despite AIM's high hopes that its occupation would mark a meaningful first step towards the reacquisition of the Black Hills, the Yellow Thunder occupation soon became a footnote in that struggle.

Leaders of the Oglala, Cheyenne River, and Rosebud Sioux tribes denounced the occupation as counter-productive. The Black Hills Sioux Nation Council withdrew its support for the Yellow Thunder Camp after less than a week. . . .

More than 100 years ago, the veteran Indian fighter General George Crook admonished the Sioux that "instead of complaining of the past, they had better think of the future." And for almost that long, it has been the policy of the United States to resolve tribal grievances in the hope that, with past accounts settled, Indians would take their place as productive and forward-looking members of American society while the nation itself would be absolved of the great sin of its expansion. During that same hundred years, the Sioux, for their part, have many times expected that their tribal claims would deliver them miraculously from the poverty and despair that followed unremittingly upon their conquest.

The story of the Black Hills claim is the story of these false hopes. There has been no cleansing of guilt on the one side, neither adjustment nor deliverance on the other.

In 1875, Chief Red Cloud announced to the whites and to his own people that the Black Hills must support the Sioux for seven generations to come. Both sides have failed him. The whites exchanged the Black Hills for a $106 million court award, sixty years in the making, a sum too little and too late even to begin the process of healing wounds that they had allowed to fester for a century.

As for the Sioux, the claims process has encouraged them to evade any real responsibility for repairing the tragic condition of their lives. They have come to believe that their status as victims, their sense of grievance, is their greatest source of strength and only hope for unity. And in this belief the Sioux have abandoned any meaningful attempt to control their own destiny in favor of rhetorical claims to sovereignty and independence.

A few lonely Sioux voices have harkened back to Red Cloud's plea—to the basic truth that without economic self-sufficiency, without a larger land base of their own, the Sioux will never again know political or spiritual freedom. In 1980, after the Supreme Court's decision in the Black Hills claim, Vine Deloria, Jr., suggested that the Sioux use their judgment money to buy land either in the Black Hills or on the existing reservations to start the process of rebuilding the tribe's economic foundation. Ramon Roubideaux has suggested that the Sioux trade their Black Hills money for federal lands in the Black Hills. Others have advised the Sioux to use their $300 million claims legacy not only to purchase land, but also to finance a massive lobbying campaign to turn around the South Dakota congressional delegation and actually secure passage of Black Hills legislation.

But these have been lonely cries in the plains wilderness. And, in the meantime, of Red Cloud's seven generations, four already have died. The fifth is dying now.

CHAPTER 4

Religious Freedom Does Not Extend to Use of Illegal Substances

Case Overview

Employment Division of Oregon v. Smith (1990)

Alfred L. Smith and Galen W. Black were drug and alcohol counselors at a nonprofit drug rehabilitation center in Oregon. Nonprescription drug use was prohibited in the terms of their employment. Black was a white man and Smith was Klamath Indian, but both men were members of the Native American Church. A central practice of the church is peyotism, the ingesting of small amounts of the hallucinogenic peyote, for sacramental purposes. When their employer learned of their peyote use, both employees were fired. Subsequently, their applications for unemployment compensation were denied by the State of Oregon's Department of Human Resources. The state said that under Oregon law employees discharged for work-related "misconduct" were not eligible for unemployment compensation. The benefits were then reinstated, only to be denied again when the Employment Appeals Board reversed its decision.

Smith appealed to the Oregon Court of Appeals, which reversed the board's decision, arguing once again that denying the unemployment benefits was proper because using peyote was a crime. The state held that the justification for withholding the benefits was outweighed by the unjustified burden imposed on Smith and Black's right of free exercise of religion. The court also rejected the Board's contention that the illegality of peyote was a factor in the case.

The Employment Division for the State of Oregon appealed to the Supreme Court. The Supreme Court said that if the state could punish the possession of peyote as a crime without infringing a person's right to exercise his religion, it could also withhold unemployment benefits from those possessing peyote without violating the right to exercise religion. However, since the Oregon Supreme Court had not relied on the fact that possession of peyote was a crime in Oregon, the U.S. Supreme Court returned the case to the lower court to determine whether or not sacramental use of illegal drugs did in fact violate the state's drug laws. The Oregon Supreme Court returned its decision saying that while Oregon drug law prohibited the consumption of illegal drugs for sacramental religious uses, this prohibition did in fact violate the free exercise clause.

The State of Oregon then appealed to the U.S. Supreme Court to review the Oregon court's second decision. *Employment Division v. Smith* was decided on April 17, 1990. In writing the majority decision, Justice Antonin Scalia observed that the Court has never held that an individual's religious beliefs excuse him from compliance with an otherwise valid law prohibiting conduct that government is free to regulate. Allowing exceptions to every state law or regulation affecting religion would, he said, "open the prospect of constitutionally required exemptions from civic obligations of almost every conceivable kind." Scalia cited as examples compulsory military service, payment of taxes, vaccination requirements, and child-neglect laws. In his dissenting opinion, Justice Harry Blackmun expressed concern for the "severe impact of a state's restrictions on the adherents of a minority religion." *Employment Division v. Smith* stunned members of religious communities, and a coalition of religious groups, which included prominent Catholic and other conservative Christian leaders, protested the Court's decision.

> "[The Court has] never held that an individual's religious beliefs excuse him from compliance with an otherwise valid law."

The Court's Decision: An Individual's Religious Beliefs Do Not Exempt Him from the Law

Antonin Scalia

Antonin Scalia has served as an associate justice of the Supreme Court since 1986. In his opinion in Employment Division of Oregon v. Smith, *he held that Oregon's prohibition of peyote use in a religious ceremony did not violate the free exercise of religion clause of the First Amendment. The state of Oregon acted constitutionally, he argues, when denying employment compensation to two members of the Native American Church who had been fired from their jobs as counselors after ingesting peyote. The two men had been fired for work-related misconduct after they were discovered to have used the hallucinogen in a religious ritual. In his written opinion, Scalia affirms that it was constitutional for Oregon to proscribe in the first place the use of sacramental peyote. General laws that do not discriminate against any particular religious practice do not violate the Constitution; because Oregon's drug laws were not targeted at the Native American church, but only incidentally penalized the Church's peyote rituals, the Constitution was not violated. Scalia asserts that Oregon would be prohibiting the free exercise of religion if*

Antonin Scalia, majority opinion, *Employment Division, Department of Human Resources of the State of Oregon, et al. v. Alfred Smith*, U.S. Supreme Court, (1990).

it sought to ban the use of peyote solely because of its religious motivation. He argues too that the First Amendment does not require that laws burdening religious exercise be justified by a compelling state interest, and in this case it was not necessary to balance the government's interest in prohibiting peyote abuse against the burden that such a prohibition places on religious practice. Scalia concludes that while it is constitutionally permissible to exempt sacramental peyote use from the operation of drug laws, it is not constitutionally required.

This case requires us to decide whether the Free Exercise Clause of the First Amendment permits the State of Oregon to include religiously inspired peyote use within the reach of its general criminal prohibition on use of that drug, and thus permits the State to deny unemployment benefits to persons dismissed from their jobs because of such religiously inspired use.

Details of the Case

Oregon law prohibits the knowing or intentional possession of a "controlled substance" unless the substance has been prescribed by a medical practitioner. The law defines "controlled substance" as a drug classified in Schedules I through V of the Federal Controlled Substances Act, as modified by the State Board of Pharmacy. Persons who violate this provision by possessing a controlled substance listed on Schedule I are "guilty of a Class B felony." As compiled by the State Board of Pharmacy under its statutory authority, Schedule I contains the drug peyote, a hallucinogen derived from the plant *Lophophora williamsii Lemaire*.

Respondents Alfred Smith and Galen Black (hereinafter respondents) were fired from their jobs with a private drug rehabilitation organization because they ingested peyote for sacramental purposes at a ceremony of the Native American Church, of which both are members. When respondents applied to petitioner Employment Division (hereinafter petitioner) for unemployment compensation, they were determined to be ineligible for benefits because they had been discharged for work-related "misconduct." The Oregon Court of Appeals reversed that determination, holding that the denial of benefits violated respondents' free exercise rights under the First Amendment.

On appeal to the Oregon Supreme Court, petitioner argued that the denial of benefits was permissible because respondents' consumption of peyote was a crime under Oregon law. The Oregon Supreme Court reasoned, however, that the criminality of respondents' peyote use was irrelevant to resolution of their constitutional claim—since the purpose of the "misconduct" provision under which respondents had been disqualified was not to enforce the State's criminal laws but to preserve the financial integrity of the compensation fund, and since that purpose was inadequate to justify the burden that disqualification imposed on respondents' religious practice. Citing our decisions in *Sherbert v. Verner*, and *Thomas v. Review Bd. of Indiana Employment Security Div.*, the court concluded that respondents were entitled to payment of unemployment benefits. We granted certiorari. . . .

Examining Precedents

Respondents' claim for relief rests on our decisions in *Sherbert v. Verner*, *Thomas v. Review Bd. of Indiana Employment Security Div.*, and *Hobbie v. Unemployment Appeals Comm'n of Florida*, in which we held that a State could not condition the availability of unemployment insurance on an individual's willingness to forgo conduct required by his religion. As we observed in *Smith I*, however, the conduct at issue in those cases was not prohibited by law. We held that distinction to be critical, for "if Oregon does prohibit the religious use of peyote, and if that prohibition is consistent with the Federal Constitution, there is no federal right to engage in that conduct in Oregon," and "the State is free to withhold unemployment compensation from respondents for engaging in work-related misconduct, despite its religious motivation." Now that the Oregon Supreme Court has confirmed that Oregon does prohibit the religious use of peyote, we proceed to consider whether that prohibition is permissible under the Free Exercise Clause.

The First Amendment and Free Exercise

The Free Exercise Clause of the First Amendment, which has been made applicable to the States by incorporation into the Fourteenth Amendment, provides that "Congress shall make no law respecting an establishment of religion, or prohibiting the free exercise thereof. . . ." The free exercise of religion means, first and foremost, the right to believe and profess whatever religious doctrine one desires. Thus, the First Amendment obviously excludes all "governmental regulation of religious beliefs as such." The government may not compel affirmation of religious belief, punish the expression of religious doctrines it believes to be false, impose special disabilities on the basis of religious views or religious status, or lend its power to one or the other side in controversies over religious authority or dogma.

But the "exercise of religion" often involves not only belief and profession but the performance of (or abstention from) physical acts: assembling with others for a worship service, participating in sacramental use of bread and wine, proselytizing, abstaining from certain foods or certain modes of transportation. It would be true, we think (though no case of ours has involved the point), that a State would be "prohibiting the free exercise [of religion]" if it sought to ban such acts or abstentions only when they are engaged in for religious reasons, or only because of the religious belief that they display. It would doubtless be unconstitutional, for example, to ban the casting of "statues that are to be used for worship purposes," or to prohibit bowing down before a golden calf.

Respondents in the present case, however, seek to carry the meaning of "prohibiting the free exercise [of religion]" one large step further. They contend that their religious motivation for using peyote places them beyond the reach of a criminal law that is not specifically directed at their religious practice, and that is concededly constitutional as applied to those who use the drug for other reasons. They assert, in other words, that "prohibiting the free exercise [of religion]" includes requiring any individual to observe a generally applicable law that requires (or forbids) the performance of an act that his religious belief forbids (or requires). As a textual matter, we do not think the words must be given that meaning. It is no more necessary to regard the collection of a general tax, for example, as "prohibiting the free exercise [of religion]" by those citizens who believe support of organized government to be sinful, than it is to regard the same tax as "abridging the freedom . . . of the press" of those publishing companies that must pay the tax as a condition of staying in business. It is a permissible reading of the text, in the one case as in the other, to say that if prohibiting the exercise of religion (or burdening the activity of printing) is not the object of the tax but merely the incidental effect of a generally applicable and otherwise valid provision, the First Amendment has not been offended.

Our decisions reveal that the latter reading is the correct one. We have never held that an individual's religious beliefs excuse him from compliance with an otherwise valid law prohibiting conduct that the State is free to regulate. On the contrary, the record of more than a century of our free exercise jurisprudence contradicts that proposition. As described succinctly by Justice [Felix] Frankfurter in *Minersville School Dist. Bd. of Ed. v. Gobitis*, "Conscientious scruples have not, in the course of the long struggle for religious toleration, relieved the individual from obedience to a general law not aimed at the promotion or restriction of religious beliefs. The mere possession of religious convictions which contradict the relevant concerns of a political society does not relieve the citizen from the discharge of political responsibilities (footnote omitted)." We first had occasion to assert that principle in *Reynolds v. United States*, where we rejected the claim that criminal laws against polygamy could not be constitutionally applied to those whose religion commanded the practice. "Laws," we said, "are made for the government of actions, and while they cannot interfere with mere religious belief and opinions, they may with practices. . . . Can a man excuse his practices to the contrary because of his religious belief? To permit this would be to make the professed doctrines of religious belief superior to the law of the land, and in effect to permit every citizen to become a law unto himself."

Neutral Laws and Religious Practices

Subsequent decisions have consistently held that the right of free exercise does not relieve an individual of the obligation to comply with a "valid and neutral law of general applicability on the ground that the law proscribes (or prescribes) conduct that his religion prescribes (or proscribes)." we held that a mother could be prosecuted under the child labor laws for using her children to dispense literature in the streets, her religious motivation notwithstanding. We found no constitutional infirmity in "excluding [these children] from doing there what no other children may do." In *Braunfeld v. Brown*, we upheld Sunday-closing laws against the claim that they burdened the religious practices of persons whose religions compelled them to refrain from work on other days. In *Gillette v. United States*, we sustained the military Selective Service System against the claim that it violated free exercise by conscripting persons who opposed a particular war on religious grounds.

Our most recent decision involving a neutral, generally applicable regulatory law that compelled activity forbidden by an individual's religion was *United States v. Lee*. There, an

Amish employer, on behalf of himself and his employees, sought exemption from collection and payment of Social Security taxes on the ground that the Amish faith prohibited participation in governmental support programs. We rejected the claim that an exemption was constitutionally required. There would be no way, we observed, to distinguish the Amish believer's objection to Social Security taxes from the religious objections that others might have to the collection or use of other taxes. "If, for example, a religious adherent believes war is a sin, and if a certain percentage of the federal budget can be identified as devoted to war-related activities, such individuals would have a similarly valid claim to be exempt from paying that percentage of the income tax. The tax system could not function if denominations were allowed to challenge the tax system because tax payments were spent in a manner that violates their religious belief."

The only decisions in which we have held that the First Amendment bars application of a neutral, generally applicable law to religiously motivated action have involved not the Free Exercise Clause alone, but the Free Exercise Clause in conjunction with other constitutional protections, such as freedom of speech and of the press. . . .

The present case does not present such a hybrid situation, but a free exercise claim unconnected with any communicative activity or parental right. Respondents urge us to hold, quite simply, that when otherwise prohibitable conduct is accompanied by religious convictions, not only the convictions but the conduct itself must be free from governmental regulation. We have never held that, and decline to do so now. There being no contention that Oregon's drug law represents an attempt to regulate religious beliefs, the communication of religious beliefs, or the raising of one's children in those beliefs, the rule to which we have adhered ever since *Reynolds* plainly controls. "Our cases do not at their farthest reach support the proposition that a stance of conscientious opposition relieves an objector from any colliding duty fixed by a democratic government."

The Test for Religious Exemption

Respondents argue that even though exemption from generally applicable criminal laws need not automatically be extended to religiously motivated actors, at least the claim for a religious exemption must be evaluated under the balancing test set forth in *Sherbert v. Verner*. Under the *Sherbert* test, governmental actions that substantially burden a religious practice must be justified by a compelling governmental interest. Applying that test we have, on three occasions, invalidated state unemployment compensation rules that conditioned the availability of benefits upon an applicant's willingness to work under conditions forbidden by his religion. We have never invalidated any governmental action on the basis of the *Sherbert* test except the denial of unemployment compensation. Although we have sometimes purported to apply the *Sherbert* test in contexts other than that, we have always found the test satisfied. In recent years we have abstained from applying the *Sherbert* test (outside the unemployment compensation field) at all. In *Bowen v. Roy*, we declined to apply *Sherbert* analysis to a federal statutory scheme that required benefit applicants and recipients to provide their Social Security numbers. The plaintiffs in that case asserted that it would violate their religious beliefs to obtain and provide a Social Security number for their daughter. We held the statute's application to the plaintiffs valid regardless of whether it was necessary to effectuate a compelling interest. In *Lyng v. Northwest Indian Cemetery Protective Assn.*, we declined to apply *Sherbert* analysis to the Government's logging and road construction activities on lands used for religious purposes by several Native American Tribes, even though it was undisputed that the activities "could have devastating effects on traditional Indian religious practices." In *Goldman v. Weinberger*, we rejected application of the *Sherbert* test to military dress regulations that forbade the wearing of yarmulkes. In *O'Lone v. Estate* of Shabazz, we sustained, without mentioning the *Sherbert* test, a prison's refusal to excuse inmates from work requirements to attend worship services.

Even if we were inclined to breathe into *Sherbert* some life beyond the unemployment compensation field, we would not apply it to require exemptions from a generally applicable criminal law. The *Shebert* test, it must be recalled, was developed in a context that lent itself to individualized governmental assessment of the reasons for the relevant conduct. As a plurality of the Court noted in *Roy*, a distinctive feature of unemployment compensation programs is that their eligibility criteria invite consideration of the particular circumstances behind an applicant's unemployment: "The statutory conditions [in *Sherbert* and *Thomas*] provided that a person was not eligible for unemployment compensation benefits if, 'without good cause,' he had quit work or refused available work. The 'good cause' standard created a mechanism for individualized exemptions." As the plurality pointed out in *Roy*, our decisions in the unemployment cases stand for the proposition that where the State has in place a system of individual exemptions, it may not refuse to extend that system to cases of "religious hardship" without compelling reason.

Whether or not the decisions are that limited, they at least have nothing to do with an across-the-board criminal prohibition on a particular form of conduct. Although, as noted earlier, we have sometimes used the *Sherbert* test to analyze free exercise challenges to such laws, we have never applied the test to invalidate one. We conclude today that the sounder approach, and the approach in accord with the vast majority of our precedents, is to hold the test inapplicable to such challenges. The government's ability to enforce generally applicable prohibitions of socially harmful conduct, like its ability to carry out other aspects of public policy, "cannot depend on measuring the effects of a governmental action on a religious objector's spiritual development." To make an individual's obligation to obey such a law contingent upon the law's coincidence with his religious beliefs, except where the State's interest is "compelling"—permitting him, by virtue of his beliefs, "to become a law unto himself," *Reynolds v. United States*, contradicts both constitutional tradition and common sense.

The "compelling government interest" requirement seems benign, because it is familiar from other fields. But using it as the standard that must be met before the government may accord different treatment on the basis of race, or before the government may regulate the content of speech, is not remotely comparable to using it for the purpose asserted here. What it produces in those other fields—equality of treatment and an unrestricted flow of contending speech—are constitutional norms; what it would produce here—a private right to ignore generally applicable laws—is a constitutional anomaly.

Nor is it possible to limit the impact of respondents' proposal by requiring a "compelling state interest" only when the conduct prohibited is "central" to the individual's religion. It is no more appropriate for judges to determine the "centrality" of religious beliefs before applying a "compelling interest" test in the free exercise field, than it would be for them to determine the "importance" of ideas before applying the "compelling interest" test in the free speech field. What principle of law or logic can be brought to bear to contradict a believer's assertion that a particular act is "central" to his personal faith? Judging the centrality of different religious practices is akin to the unacceptable "business of evaluating the relative merits of differing religious claims." As we reaffirmed only last Term, "[i]t is not within the judicial ken to question the centrality of particular beliefs or practices to a faith, or the validity of particular litigants' interpretations of those creeds." Repeatedly and in many different contexts, we have warned that courts must not presume to determine the place of a particular belief in a religion or the plausibility of a religious claim.

Religious Freedom and the Political Process

If the "compelling interest" test is to be applied at all, then, it must be applied across the board, to all actions thought to be religiously commanded. Moreover, if "compelling interest" really means what it says (and watering it down here would subvert its rigor in the other fields where it is applied), many laws will not meet the test. Any society adopting such a system would be courting anarchy, but that danger increases in direct proportion to the society's diversity of religious beliefs, and its determination to coerce or suppress none of them. Precisely because "we are a cosmopolitan nation made up of people of almost every conceivable religious preference," and precisely because we value and protect that religious divergence, we cannot afford the luxury of deeming presumptively invalid, as applied to the religious objector, every regulation of conduct that does not protect an interest of the highest order. The rule respondents favor would open the prospect of constitutionally required religious exemptions from civic obligations of almost every conceivable kind—ranging from compulsory military service, to the payment of taxes, to health and safety regulation such as manslaughter and child neglect laws, compulsory vaccination laws, drug laws, and traffic laws, social welfare legislation such as minimum wage laws, child labor laws, animal cruelty laws, environmental protection laws, and laws providing for equality of opportunity for the races. The First Amendment's protection of religious liberty does not require this.

Values that are protected against government interference through enshrinement in the Bill of Rights are not thereby banished from the political process. Just as a society that believes in the negative protection accorded to the press by the First Amendment is likely to enact laws that affirmatively foster the dissemination of the printed word, so also a society that believes in the negative protection accorded to religious belief can be expected to be solicitous of that value in its legislation as well. It is therefore not surprising that a number of States have made an exception to their drug laws for sacramental peyote use.

But to say that a nondiscriminatory religious-practice exemption is permitted, or even that it is desirable, is not to say that it is constitutionally required, and that the appropriate occasions for its creation can be discerned by the courts. It may fairly be said that leaving accommodation to the political process will place at a relative disadvantage those religious practices that are not widely engaged in; but that unavoidable consequence of democratic government must be preferred to a system in which each conscience is a law unto itself or in which judges weigh the social importance of all laws against the centrality of all religious beliefs.

Because respondents' ingestion of peyote was prohibited under Oregon law, and because that prohibition is constitutional, Oregon may, consistent with the Free Exercise Clause, deny respondents unemployment compensation when their dismissal results from use of the drug. The decision of the Oregon Supreme Court is accordingly reversed.

> *"This Court must scrupulously apply its free exercise analysis to the religious claims of Native Americans, no matter how unorthodox they may be."*

Dissenting Opinion: First Amendment Values Protect "Unorthodox" Religious Practices

Harry Blackmun

Harry Blackmun was an associate justice of the Supreme Court from 1970 to 1994. In his dissenting opinion in the matter of Employment Division of Oregon v. Smith, *Blackmun rejected Justice Antonin Scalia's decision that a state is acting within its constitutional rights to deny unemployment benefits to someone who has used peyote for sacramental purposes. Blackmun feared "the severe impact of a state's restrictions on the adherents of a minority religion." He understands eating peyote to be "an act of worship and communion" and a "means for communicating with the Great Spirit." Blackmun felt it inconsistent with First Amendment values to denigrate an "unorthodox" religious practice by creating a hostile environment in which it could not be practiced freely.*

This Court over the years painstakingly has developed a consistent and exacting standard to test the constitutionality of a state statute that burdens the free exercise of religion. Such a statute may stand only if the law in general, and

Harry Blackmun, dissenting opinion, *Employment Division, Department of Human Resources of the State of Oregon, et al. v. Alfred Smith*, U.S. Supreme Court, (1990).

the State's refusal to allow a religious exemption in particular, are justified by a compelling interest that cannot be served by less restrictive means.

Until today, I thought this was a settled and inviolate principle of this Court's First Amendment jurisprudence. The majority, however, perfunctorily dismisses it as a "constitutional anomaly." As carefully detailed in Justice [Sandra Day] O'Connor's concurring opinion, the majority is able to arrive at this view only by mischaracterizing this Court's precedents. The Court discards leading free exercise cases such as *Cantwell v. Connecticut*, and *Wisconsin v. Yoder*, as "hybrid." The Court views traditional free exercise analysis as somehow inapplicable to criminal prohibitions (as opposed to conditions on the receipt of benefits), and to state laws of general applicability (as opposed, presumably, to laws that expressly single out religious practices). The Court cites cases in which, due to various exceptional circumstances, we found strict scrutiny inapposite, to hint that the Court has repudiated that standard altogether. . . . In short, it effectuates a wholesale overturning of settled law concerning the Religion Clauses of our Constitution. One hopes that the Court is aware of the consequences, and that its result is not a product of overreaction to the serious problems the country's drug crisis has generated.

This distorted view of our precedents leads the majority to conclude that strict scrutiny of a state law burdening the free exercise of religion is a "luxury" that a well-ordered society cannot afford, and that the repression of minority religions is an "unavoidable consequence of democratic government." I do not believe the Founders thought their dearly bought freedom from religious persecution a "luxury," but an essential element of liberty—and they could not have thought religious intolerance "unavoidable," for they drafted the Religion Clauses precisely in order to avoid that intolerance.

For these reasons, I agree with Justice O'Connor's analysis of the applicable free exercise doctrine, and I join parts I and

II of her opinion. As she points out, "the critical question in this case is whether exempting respondents from the State's general criminal prohibition 'will unduly interfere with fulfillment of the governmental interest.'" I do disagree, however, with her specific answer to that question.

What Is the State's Interest?

In weighing the clear interest of respondents [Alfred] Smith and [Galen] Black (hereinafter respondents) in the free exercise of their religion against Oregon's asserted interest in enforcing its drug laws, it is important to articulate in precise terms the state interest involved. It is not the State's broad interest in fighting the critical "war on drugs" that must be weighed against respondents' claim, but the State's narrow interest in refusing to make an exception for the religious, ceremonial use of peyote.... Failure to reduce the competing interests to the same plane of generality tends to distort the weighing process in the State's favor....

The State's interest in enforcing its prohibition, in order to be sufficiently compelling to outweigh a free exercise claim, cannot be merely abstract or symbolic. The State cannot plausibly assert that unbending application of a criminal prohibition is essential to fulfill any compelling interest, if it does not, in fact, attempt to enforce that prohibition. In this case, the State actually has not evinced any concrete interest in enforcing its drug laws against religious users of peyote. Oregon has never sought to prosecute respondents, and does not claim that it has made significant enforcement efforts against other religious users of peyote. The State's asserted interest thus amounts only to the symbolic preservation of an unenforced prohibition. But a government interest in "symbolism, even symbolism for so worthy a cause as the abolition of unlawful drugs," cannot suffice to abrogate the constitutional rights of individuals.

Similarly, this Court's prior decisions have not allowed a government to rely on mere speculation about potential harms, but have demanded evidentiary support for a refusal to allow a religious exception.... In this case, the State's justification for refusing to recognize an exception to its criminal laws for religious peyote use is entirely speculative.

The War on Drugs

The State proclaims an interest in protecting the health and safety of its citizens from the dangers of unlawful drugs. It offers, however, no evidence that the religious use of peyote has ever harmed anyone. The factual findings of other courts cast doubt on the State's assumption that religious use of peyote is harmful....

The fact that peyote is classified as a Schedule I controlled substance does not, by itself, show that any and all uses of peyote, in any circumstance, are inherently harmful and dangerous. The Federal Government, which created the classifications of unlawful drugs from which Oregon's drug laws are derived, apparently does not find peyote so dangerous as to preclude an exemption for religious use....

The carefully circumscribed ritual context in which respondents used peyote is far removed from the irresponsible and unrestricted recreational use of unlawful drugs. The Native American Church's internal restrictions on, and supervision of, its members' use of peyote substantially obviate the State's health and safety concerns....

Moreover, just as in *Yoder*, the values and interests of those seeking a religious exemption in this case are congruent, to a great degree, with those the State seeks to promote through its drug laws.... No only does the church's doctrine forbid nonreligious use of peyote; it also generally advocates self-reliance, familial responsibility, and abstinence from alcohol.... There is considerable evidence that the spiritual and social support provided by the church has been effective in combating the tragic effects of alcoholism on the Native American population. Two noted experts on peyotism, Dr. Omer C. Stewart and Dr. Robert Bergman, testified by affidavit to this effect on behalf of respondent Smith before the Employment Appeal Board. . . . Far from promoting the lawless and irresponsible use of drugs, Native American Church members' spiritual code exemplifies values that Oregon's drug laws are presumably intended to foster.

The State also seeks to support its refusal to make an exception for religious use of peyote by invoking its interest in abolishing drug trafficking. There is, however, practically no illegal traffic in peyote. Also, the availability of peyote for religious use, even if Oregon were to allow an exemption from its criminal laws, would still be strictly controlled by federal regulations, and by the State of Texas, the only State in which peyote grows in significant quantities. Peyote simply is not a popular drug; its distribution for use in religious rituals has nothing to do with the vast and violent traffic in illegal narcotics that plagues this country.

Finally, the State argues that granting an exception for religious peyote use would erode its interest in the uniform, fair, and certain enforcement of its drug laws. The State fears that, if it grants an exemption for religious peyote use, a flood of other claims to religious exemptions will follow. It would then be placed in a dilemma, it says, between allowing a patchwork of exemptions that would hinder its law enforcement efforts, and risking a violation of the Establishment Clause by arbitrarily limiting its religious exemptions. This argument, however, could be made in almost any free exercise case. This Court, however, consistently has rejected similar arguments in past free exercise cases, and it should do so here as well.

The State's apprehension of a flood of other religious claims is purely speculative. Almost half the States, and the Federal Government, have maintained an exemption for religious peyote use for many years, and apparently have not found themselves overwhelmed by claims to other religious exemptions. Allowing an exemption for religious peyote use would not necessarily oblige the State to grant a similar exemption to other religious groups. The unusual circumstances that make the religious use of peyote compatible with the State's interests in health and safety and in preventing drug trafficking would not apply to other religious claims. Some religions, for example, might not restrict drug use to a limited ceremonial context, as does the Native American Church. Some religious claims, involve drugs such as marijuana and heroin, in which there is significant illegal traffic, with its attendant greed and violence, so that it would be difficult to grant a religious exemption without seriously compromising law enforcement efforts. That the State might grant an exemption for religious peyote use, but deny other religious claims arising in different circumstances, would not violate the Establishment Clause. Though the State must treat all religions equally, and not favor one over another, this obligation is fulfilled by the uniform application of the "compelling interest" test to all free exercise claims, not by reaching uniform results as to all claims. A showing that religious peyote use does not unduly interfere with the State's interests is "one that probably few other religious groups or sects could make," this does not mean that an exemption limited to peyote use is tantamount to an establishment of religion. . . .

Restrictions on Unorthodox Religion

Finally, although I agree with Justice O'Connor that courts should refrain from delving into questions whether, as a matter of religious doctrine, a particular practice is "central" to the religion, . . . I do not think this means that the courts must turn a blind eye to the severe impact of a State's restrictions on the adherents of a minority religion.

Respondents believe, and their sincerity has never been at issue, that the peyote plant embodies their deity, and eating it is an act of worship and communion. Without peyote, they could not enact the essential ritual of their religion.

If Oregon can constitutionally prosecute them for this act of worship, they, like the Amish, may be "forced to migrate to some other and more tolerant region." This potentially devastating impact must be viewed in light of the federal policy—reached in reaction to many years of religious persecution and intolerance—of protecting the religious freedom of Native Americans. Congress recognized that certain substances, such as peyote, "have religious significance because they are sacred, they have power, they heal, they are necessary to the exercise of the rites of the religion, they are necessary to the cultural integrity of the tribe, and, therefore, religious survival."

The American Indian Religious Freedom Act, in itself, may not create rights enforceable against government action restricting religious freedom, but this Court must scrupulously apply its free exercise analysis to the religious claims of Native Americans, however unorthodox they may be. Otherwise, both the First Amendment and the stated policy of Congress will offer to Native Americans merely an unfulfilled and hollow promise.

For these reasons, I conclude that Oregon's interest in enforcing its drug laws against religious use of peyote is not sufficiently compelling to outweigh respondents' right to the free exercise of their religion. Since the State could not constitutionally enforce its criminal prohibition against respondents, the interests underlying the State's drug laws cannot justify its denial of unemployment benefits. Absent such justification, the State's regulatory interest in denying benefits for religiously motivated "misconduct," is indistinguishable from the state interests this Court has rejected in *Frazee, Hobbie, Thomas*, and *Sherbert*. The State of Oregon cannot, consistently with the Free Exercise Clause, deny respondents unemployment benefits.

I dissent.

> *"All [religious groups] agreed that the opinion was 'disastrous for the free exercise of religion.'"*

Religious Leaders and Scholars Criticize the *Smith* Ruling

Linda Greenhouse

Linda Greenhouse covers the United States Supreme Court for the New York Times. *In the following article, she reports on the request by a diverse coalition of religious groups and constitutional scholars that the Supreme Court reconsider their decision in the* Employment Division of Oregon v. Smith *case, which affirmed the constitutionality of Oregon's refusing employment benefits to persons who use illegal drugs as part of religious rituals. The coalition—made up of such diverse groups as the American Jewish Congress, the National Council of Churches, the American Friends Service Committee, the General Conference of Seventh-Day Adventists, the American Civil Liberties Union, and the Rutherford Institute—hoped if not to reverse the decision to at least make the public and the Court aware of the widespread dismay that the opinion had provoked. The Supreme Court later declined the petition to reconsider the case.*

A n unusually diverse coalition of religious groups and constitutional scholars asked the Supreme Court today [May 10, 1990,] to reconsider a recent decision permitting states to take legal action against people who use illegal drugs as part of religious rituals.

173

The petition requesting the rehearing told the Justices that "every religious group in the country will be profoundly disadvantaged" by the "far-reaching holding" issued [in April 1990]. The request was made on behalf of two members of an American Indian church in which the ceremonial use of the hallucinogenic cactus peyote has been an important sacrament for centuries.

The 5-to-4 opinion in *Employment Division v. Smith*, written by Justice Antonin Scalia, rejected the Indians' argument that their use of peyote was protected by the First Amendment's guarantee of the free exercise of religion.

The opinion said the guarantee did not generally exempt a person from complying with a valid law, even if the law conflicted with a religious belief.

Rehearings Are Rarely Granted

Requests for rehearings are filed frequently by the losing side, but the Supreme Court rarely grants them. Not since the early 1960's have the Justices agreed to reconsider a case.

Oliver S. Thomas, general counsel of the Baptist Joint Committee on Public Affairs, one of the groups supporting the effort, said at a news conference that there was only an outside chance that the Court would grant the request. "But it's our only shot, so we take it," he said.

Mr. Thomas and several other lawyers said the coalition hoped at least to make both the public and the Court aware of the dismay that the opinion had provoked.

Among the 15 other organizations participating were the American Jewish Congress, the National Council of Churches, the National Association of Evangelicals, the American Friends Service Committee and the General Conference of Seventh-Day Adventists. Public interest groups not affiliated with religious denominations also joined the effort, including the American Civil Liberties Union and People for the American Way on the liberal side, and the Rutherford Institute on the conservative side.

Diverse Groups All Agree

"I seriously doubt that these groups have ever been in the same room together," Mr. Thomas said, adding that they all agreed that the opinion was "disastrous for the free exercise of religion."

Among the 55 constitutional scholars who signed the petition were Gerald Gunther of Stanford Law School, Laurence H. Tribe of Harvard Law School, Norman Redlich of New York University Law School, Sanford Levinson and Douglas Laycook of the University of Texas Law School, Kent Greenawalt of Columbia Law School and Michael W. McConnell of the University of Chicago Law School.

The focus of the coalition's concern was not so much the outcome of the case as the Court's analysis. Justice Scalia's opinion rejected the principle, included in several of the Court's earlier decisions on the subject, that a governmental action that places a burden on religious observance is unconstitutional unless it serves a "compelling state interest."

Both sides in the case had assumed that the "compelling state interest" analysis would govern the outcome. Oregon had denied unemployment benefits to the two plaintiffs because they had been dismissed from their jobs for using peyote. The state argued that its interest in enforcing narcotics laws uniformly was "compelling." The Indians argued that it was not.

Matter for Politics, Not Courts

But Justice Scalia said the Court's precedents applying compelling state interest "have nothing to do with an across-the-board criminal prohibition on a particular form of conduct." He said American society would be "courting anarchy" if the Court endorsed the approach of granting "constitutionally required religious exemptions from civic obligations of almost every conceivable kind."

Noting that the Federal Government and many state legislatures had already exempted sacramental peyote from their narcotics laws, Justice Scalia said "the political process," not the courts, should make such choices.

In the petition asking for a rehearing, the coalition warned that such an analysis would permit the Government to ban as non-humane the ritual slaughter required under Jewish law to make meat kosher, the circumcisions practiced by Jews and Moslems, or the use of wine in the Roman Catholic Mass.

The petition, prepared by lawyers for Oregon Legal Services and the American Jewish Congress, told the Court that rehearing was necessary because none of the briefs in the peyote case had even considered the prospect that the compelling state interest test would not be applied.

Rehearing Requires a Majority

Under the Court's rules, a majority must agree for a case to be reheard.

Justice Scalia's opinion was joined by Chief Justice William H. Rehnquist and Justices Byron R. White, John Paul Stevens and Anthony M. Kennedy.

Justice Sandra Day O'Connor cast a sixth vote in support of the state's position, saying that Oregon had "a compelling interest in regulating peyote use by its citizens." But she refused to join Justice Scalia's opinion, labeling it "incompatible with our nation's fundamental commitment to individual religious liberty."

Even if Justice O'Connor supported a rehearing request, however, it would still need the support of at least one of the Justices in the majority.

The Court is likely to act on the request in the next several weeks.

The last case the Court reconsidered was *Flora v. U.S.*, which held that Federal district courts could not hear certain tax refund suits. After the rehearing in 1960, the Court reaffirmed its initial decision, issued in 1958.

But in 1957, a reargument changed the outcome of a case. The Court ruled after rehearing *Reid v. Covert* that the military does not have court-martial jurisdiction over civilians in peacetime. The initial decision, in 1956, had gone the other way.

"*[The* Smith *ruling] is yet another stark testimony to the difficulty tribal nations have experienced in their quest for permanent recognition of their unique . . . traditions.*"

Smith Sparked Legislative Action

David Wilkins

David E. Wilkins is a professor of American Indian studies, political science, law, and American studies at the University of Minnesota. In the following article, he argues that Employment Division of Oregon v. Smith *should have been considered moot because the issue had already been resolved before going to the Supreme Court. The defendants, Alfred Smith and Galen Black, had been fired from their jobs as drug counselors after ingesting peyote at a Native American Church ritual. In his deciding opinion, Justice Antonin Scalia had upheld the ruling of the Oregon Supreme Court that the state was justified in denying the two men's unemployment compensation claims because they were dismissed for work-related "misconduct." Wilkins explains why the case was resuscitated after it was considered dead and explores the justifications offered by Scalia for his decision. He also discusses the effect of the* Smith *verdict on freedom of religion in general and the rights of Indians specifically to practice their unique cultural and religious traditions.*

David Wilkins, *American Indian Sovereignty and the U.S. Supreme Court: The Masking of Justice*. Austin: University of Texas Press, 1997, pp. 235–96. Copyright © 1997 by the University of Texas Press. All rights reserved. Reproduced by permission of the University of Texas Press.

Antonin Scalia's excising of the Free Exercise Clause [from his decision in *Employment Division of Oregon v. Smith*] meant that the exercise of religion, notwithstanding what the Constitution said, deserved no special protection, and American Indians and tribes had another defeat to add to their scrap heap of trampled rights. Scalia's reasoning in this decision harks back to [Justice] Felix S. Cohen's oft-quoted statement of 1949 that "for us [Euro-Americans], the Indian tribe is the miners' canary and when it flutters and droops we know that the poison gases of intolerance threaten all of the minorities in our land. And who of us is not a member of some minority?"

In the wake of *Smith*, a diverse coalition of religious groups and constitutional scholars, after carefully assessing the revolutionary impact of this case, confronted the Supreme Court and asked it to reconsider its decision. The petition said that "every religious group in the country will be profoundly disadvantaged" by this "far-reaching holding." Among the fifteen or so organizations jointly involved in the petition for the rehearing, only a few represented religious minorities, and no Indian groups were included. The American Jewish Congress, the National Association of Evangelicals, the American Friends Service Committee, and the General Conference of Seventh Day Adventists teamed up with the National Council of Churches and nonreligious public interest groups including the American Civil Liberties Union and People for the American Way on the liberal side, and the Rutherford Institute on the conservative side. Moreover, fifty-five constitutional scholars signed the petition. This rehearing request, like all others since the early 1960s, was rejected. The anti-*Smith* coalition persisted, however, turning their focus to Congress where they found leaders willing to introduce legislation that would reestablish the compelling governmental interest standard.

Tribal individuals and their governments also reacted swiftly to *Smith*. In the early eighties, they had formed an organization called the American Indian Religious Freedom Coalition (AIRFC), which had sought amendments to the weak American Indian Religious Freedom Act. Supported by concerned congressional representatives, various Christian denominations, and a number of Indian and non-Indian lobbying interest groups and organizations, they vigorously sought legislative action to counter the destructive effects of both *Lyng* [*v. Northwest Indian CPA*] and *Smith*. Tribes and their supporters were buoyed by their success in securing enactment of a 1991 law which overturned a major criminal law case, *Duro v. Reina* (1990). *Duro* had deprived tribal governments of the right to exercise misdemeanor criminal jurisdiction over nonmember Indians.

Broad legislation to reconstruct the compelling interest test, called the "Religious Freedom Reformation Act of 1993," was enacted on November 16, 1993. It explicitly restored the compelling interest test as originally set forth in *Sherbert v. Verner* and *Wisconsin v. Yoder*. It also guaranteed application of the test in all cases where free exercise of religion is substantially burdened, and it provided a claim or defense to persons whose religious exercise is substantially burdened by government. Section 3 of the law says, "[G]overnment shall not substantially burden a person's exercise of religion even if the burden results from a rule of general applicability, except as provided in Subsection B." The exception is when the government is acting "in furtherance of a compelling governmental interest" and where the government's action "is the least restrictive means of furthering that compelling governmental interest."

The focus of the AIRFC became dramatically intensified and sharpened after *Lyng* and *Smith*. An omnibus Indian religious freedom bill was introduced July 1, 1994, by Senator Daniel Inouye (D., Hawaii). Entitled the "Native American Cultural Protection and Free Exercise of Religion Act" (S. 2269), it would not only address the Court's anti-peyote *Smith* precedent, it would also, and more importantly, charter new federal policy designed to provide religious protection for tribal people in three other areas: sacred sites, Indian prisoners' rights, and religious use of eagles and animal parts. Moreover, the bill contained enforcement mechanisms which the original 1978 resolution had lacked. Such legislation would have provided American Indians with substantial religious rights. Although this omnibus legislation failed, a separate bill, H.R. 4230, which focused solely on peyote, was enacted into law on October 6, 1994. Entitled the "American Indian Religious Freedom Act Amendments of 1994," this measure rebuffed *Smith* and legalized the use of peyote so long as it was connected with the practice of traditional Indian religions.

In effect, two related but distinctive legislative thrusts were underway—the legislation being pushed by the largely non-Indian movement seeking restoration of the compelling interest test; and the AIRFC-inspired legislation which had a broader goal of recognizing traditional Indian religious rights. While some members of Congress questioned the need for separate bills, one for Native Americans and another for all other religions, Senator Paul Wellstone (D., Minnesota), a co-sponsor of the 1993 version of the Indian religion bill, put it best in addressing this issue:

> Throughout the series of hearings held around the country on NAFERA [Native American Free Exercise of Religion Act] one theme repeated itself over and over again: our traditional understanding of how to protect religious freedom, based on a European understanding of religion, is insufficient to protect the rights of the first Americans. . . . The question is not, should we protect Indian religious freedom? Instead, we must ask, how can we best live up to our obligation to protect that freedom? This is an important question, because one might legitimately want to ask why we need a bill to address specifically the religious freedom of Native Americans, instead of a bill that addresses all religions at one time. There is, of course, such a bill, the Religious Free-

dom Restoration Act (RFRA), which has recently been introduced by my colleague from Massachusetts, Senator [Edward] Kennedy, and of which I am an original co-sponsor. I believe that there is a strong argument to be made that both of these bills ought to be made into law. RFRA is designed to respond in a very general way to judicial decisions that have been made in recent years restricting the right to free practice of religion. . . . But leaving the definition of such standards up to the judiciary has not proven very effective for Native American religions. In NAFERA, on the other hand, we provide language that makes clear the particularities of Native religious practices we intend to address.

Conclusion

The more comprehensive Indian religious bill, excluding the peyote aspect, which was directly aimed at the protection of all traditional Indian religions, was never enacted, while the Religious Freedom Restoration Act (RFRA), which was supported by western religions, did become law. This failure is yet another stark testimony to the difficulty tribal nations have experienced in their quest for permanent recognition of their unique religious and cultural traditions.

Though Indian tribes and individuals were on the receiving end of three disastrous Supreme Court decisions involving religion—*Bowen* [*v. Roy*], *Lyng*, and *Smith*—which sparked a successful counterrevolution of religious organizations and constitutional scholars, American Indian tribal nations who practice traditional religions that do not involve the use of peyote have yet to receive the basic constitutional protection which has been legislatively "restored" for other Americans under the RFRA and for the use of peyote under the AIRFA.

Organizations to Contact

The editors have compiled the following list of organizations concerned with the issues debated in this book. The descriptions are derived from materials provided by the organizations. All have publications or information available for interested readers. The list was compiled on the date of publication of the present volume; the information provided here may change. Be aware that many organizations take several weeks or longer to respond to inquiries, so allow as much time as possible.

American Indian Movement (AIM)
PO Box 134, Federal Dam, MN   56641
Web site: www.aimovement.org

The American Indian Movement is a civil rights movement founded in 1968. Its purpose is to encourage self-determination among Native Americans and to establish international recognition of their treaty rights. AIM has repeatedly brought successful lawsuits against the federal government for the protection of the rights of Native Nations guaranteed in treaties, sovereignty, the United States Constitution, and laws. The philosophy of self-determination upon which the movement is built is deeply rooted in traditional spirituality, culture, language, and history. AIM also develops partnerships to address the common needs of the people.

The American Indian Rights and Resources Organization (AIRRO)
41801 Corte Valentine, Temecula, CA   92592
(951) 694-6264
Web site: www.airro.org

The American Indian Rights and Resources Organization was founded to educate and assist all individuals regarding basic human and civil rights issues. AIRRO serves as a resource for those seeking information or assistance regarding the Indian

Civil Rights Act of 1968 and other laws that impact the human rights and civil liberties of American Indians and non-Indian individuals. AIRRO also works to assist individuals in order to protect, promote, and preserve their basic human rights and civil liberties and to effect change that ensures equal rights and equal protections for all.

Bureau of Indian Affairs
Department of the Interior, 1849 C St. NW
Washington, DC   20240
Web site: www.doi.gov/bureau-indian-affairs.html

The Bureau of Indian Affairs was set up in 1842 and from the beginning had jurisdiction over trade with Native Americans, their removal to the West, their protection from exploitation, and their concentration on reservations. Today the agency is responsible for the administration and management of 55.7 million acres of land held in trust by the United States for American Indians and Alaska Natives. Developing forestlands; leasing assets on these lands; directing agricultural programs; protecting water and land rights; and developing and maintaining infrastructure and economic development are all part of the agency's responsibility.

Citizens Equal Rights Alliance (CERA)
PO Box 1280, Toppenish, WA   98948
(509) 865-6225 • fax: (509) 865-7409
Web site: www.citizensalliance.org

The Citizens Equal Rights Alliance calls for limiting Indian sovereignty and protecting the rights of whites and other non-Indians on tribal lands. CERA declares that federal Indian policy is unaccountable, destructive, racist, and unconstitutional, and it therefore seeks to ensure equal protection under the law as guaranteed to all citizens by the Constitution of the United States. The alliance holds that all people in the United States should be subject to the same laws and one government, and that Native Americans should not be granted sovereignty over the land that was taken from them.

The Indian Law Resource Center
602 N. Ewing St., Helena, MT   59601
(406) 449-2006

The Indian Law Resource Center is a nonprofit law and advocacy organization established and directed by American Indians. It provides legal assistance to Indian and Alaska Native
nations that are working to protect their lands, resources, human rights, environment, and cultural heritage. The center's
principal goal is the preservation and well-being of Indian
and other native nations and tribes.

Midwest Treaty Network (MTN)
PO Box 43, Oneida, WI   54155
(920) 496-5360 or (715) 295-0018
Web site: www.treatyland.com

The Midwest Treaty Network was founded in 1989 as an alliance of Indian and non-Indian groups supporting Native
American sovereignty in the western Great Lakes region. The
group was founded in response to the Wisconsin Chippewa
(Ojibwe) spearfishing crisis in the 1980s but got involved in
backing sovereignty, treaty rights, and cultural and environmental protection of other indigenous nations throughout the
region. The MTN emphasizes public education, grassroots action, and finding common ground between Indian and non-
Indian communities.

National Tribal Justice Resource Center
4410 Arapahoe Ave., Suite 135, Boulder, Colorado   80303
(303) 245-0786
Web site: www.tribalresourcecenter.org

The National Tribal Justice Resource Center is the largest and
most comprehensive site dedicated to tribal justice systems,
personnel, and tribal law. The center is the central national
clearinghouse of information for Native American and Alaska
Native tribal courts, providing both technical assistance and
resources for the development and enhancement of tribal jus-

tice system personnel. Programs and services developed by the center are offered to all tribal justice system personnel—whether working with formalized tribal courts or with tradition-based tribal dispute resolution forums.

Native American Rights Fund (NARF)
1506 Broadway, Boulder, CO   80302-6296
(303) 447-8760 • fax: (303) 443-7776
Web site: www.narf.org

The Native American Rights Fund is a nonprofit organization that provides legal representation and technical assistance to Indian tribes, organizations, and individuals nationwide—a constituency that often lacks access to the justice system. NARF focuses on applying existing laws and treaties to guarantee that national and state governments live up to their legal obligations.

For Further Research

Books

William C. Canby, *American Indian Law in a Nutshell.* St. Paul: West, 2004.

Blue Clark, Lone Wolf v. Hitchcock: *Treaty Rights and Indian Law at the End of the Nineteenth Century.* Lincoln: University of Nebraska Press, 1999.

Vine Deloria Jr., *Behind the Trail of Broken Treaties: An Indian Declaration of Independence.* Austin: University of Texas Press, 1985.

Vine Deloria and Clifford M. Lytle, *American Indians, American Justice.* Austin: University of Texas Press, 1983.

Vine Deloria and Clifford M. Lytle, *The Nations Within: The Past and Future of American Indian Sovereignty.* Austin: University of Texas Press, 1998.

Vine Deloria and David E. Wilkins, *Tribes, Treaties, and Constitutional Tribulations.* Austin: University of Texas Press, 2000.

N. Bruce Duthu and Colin Calloway, *American Indians and the Law.* The Penguin Library of American Indian History. New York: Viking, 2008.

David H. Getches, Charles F. Wilkinson, and Robert A. Williams, *Cases and Materials on Federal Indian Law.* St. Paul: West, 2004.

Allen Guttmann, *States' Rights and Indian Removal:* The Cherokee Nation v. the State of Georgia. Boston: D.C. Heath, 1965.

Alvin M. Josephy, *The Indian Heritage of America.* Boston: Mariner, 1991.

Edward Lazarus, *Black Hills, White Justice: The Sioux Nation Versus the United States, 1775 to the Present*. New York: HarperPerennial, 2002.

Peter Nabokov, ed., *Native American Testimony: A Chronicle of Indian-White Relations from Prophecy to the Present, 1942–2000*. New York: Penguin, 1999.

Jill Norgren, *Cherokee Cases: Two Landmark Federal Decisions in the Fight for Sovereignty*. Norman: University of Oklahoma Press, 1992.

Wendell H. Oswalt, *This Land Was Theirs: A Study of Native North Americans*. New York: Oxford University Press, 2005.

Stephen L. Pevar, *The Rights of Indians and Tribes: The Authoritative ACLU Guide to Indian and Tribal Rights*. New York: New York University Press, 2004.

Charles P. Townsend, *Native Americans: Rights, Laws and Legislative Developments*. Hauppauge, NY: Nova Science, 2008.

David E. Wilkins and K. Tsianina Lomawaima, *Uneven Ground: American Indian Sovereignty and Federal Law*. Norman: University of Oklahoma Press, 2002.

Periodicals

General

Edward A. Adams, "Whose Land Is It, Anyway?" *National Law Journal*, August 3, 1987.

Amanda J. Cobb, "Understanding Tribal Sovereignty: Definitions, Conceptualizations, and Interpretations," *American Studies*, Fall/Winter 2005.

Robert Ericson and D. Rebecca Snow, "The Indian Battle for Self-Determination," *California Law Review*, March 1970.

David H. Getches, "Conquering the Cultural Frontier: The New Subjectivism of the Supreme Court in Indian Law," *California Law Review*, December 1996.

John R. Hermann, "American Indians in Court: The Burger and Rehnquist Years," *Social Science Journal*, April 2000.

Carol Chiago Lujan and Gordon Adams, "U.S. Colonization of Indian Justice Systems: A Brief History," *Wicazo Sa Review*, Autumn 2004.

Cherokee Nation v. Georgia

Ronald A. Berutti, "The Cherokee Cases: The Fight to Save the Supreme Court and the Cherokee Indians," *American Indian Law Review* Spring 1992.

Stephen G. Breyer, "'For Their Own Good'—The Cherokees, the Supreme Court, and the Early History of American Conscience," *New Republic*, August 7, 2000.

Norman Finkelstein, "History's Verdict: The Cherokee Case," *Journal of Palestine Studies*, Summer 1995.

New York Times, "Georgia to Pardon Two in 1831 Case; Men Were Jailed for Fighting Seizure of Cherokee Land," November 23, 1992.

David E. Wilkins, "The U.S. Supreme Court's Explication of 'Federal Plenary Power': An Analysis of Case Law Affecting Tribal Sovereignty, 1886–1914," *American Indian Quarterly*, Summer 1994.

Lone Wolf v. Hitchcock

Philip P. Frickey, "Doctrine, Context, Institutional Relationships, and Commentary: The Malaise of Federal Indian Law Through the Lens of *Lone Wolf*," *Tulsa Law Review*, Fall 2002.

Frank Pommersheim, "*Lone Wolf v. Hitchcock*: A Little Haiku Essay on a Missed Constitutional Moment," *Tulsa Law Review*, Fall 2002.

Catherine Elliott Shreves, "The Demise of *Lone Wolf v. Hitchcock* in Fifth Amendment Tribal Land Claim Cases," *South Dakota Law Review*, Summer 1981.

Bryan H. Wildenthal, "Fighting the *Lone Wolf* Mentality: Twenty-first Century Reflections on the Paradoxical State of American Indian Law," *Tulsa Law Review*, Fall 2002.

Kathryn C. Wyatt, "The Supreme Court, *Lyng*, and the *Lone Wolf* Principle," *Chicago-Kent Law Review*, Spring 1989.

United States v. Sioux Nation

Ward Churchill, "The Black Hills Are Not for Sale: A Summary of the Lakota Struggle for the 1868 Treaty Territory," *Journal of Ethnic Studies*, Spring 1990.

Marc Goldstein, "Dilemma for the Sioux: Take Money or Fight?" *New York Times*, July 16, 1984.

Anthony G. Gulig and Sidney L. Harring, "Federal Plenary Power in Indian Affairs After *Weeks* and *Sioux Nation*," *University of Pennsylvania Law Review*, November 1982.

Jill E. Martin, "Returning the Black Hills," *Journal of the West*, Summer 2000.

Frank Pommersheim, "The Black Hills Case: On the Cusp of History," *Wicazo Sa Review*, Spring 1988.

————— "Black Hills, White Justice: The Sioux Nation Versus the United States, 1775 to the Present." *North Dakota Law Review*, Spring 1993.

Employment Division of Oregon v. Smith

Robert N. Clinton, "Peyote and Judicial Political Activism; Neo-colonialism and the Supreme Court's New Indian Law Agenda," *Federal Bar News & Journal*, March 1991.

Economist, "Must Say No," October 6, 1990.

Elena Neuman, "Moving the Line Between Church and State," *Insight on the News*, May 18, 1992.

New York Times, "For 2, an Answer to Years of Doubt on Ritual Use of Peyote," July 9, 1991.

Mordecai Specktor, "American Indians, Panel Discuss Religious Law," *National Catholic Reporter*, March 26, 1993.

Mike Townsend, "Congressional Abrogation of Indian Treaties: Reevaluation and Reform," *Yale Law Journal*, February 1989.

Priscilla Wald, "Terms of Assimilation: Legislating Subjectivity in the Emerging Nation," *Boundary,* Fall 1992.

David E. Wilkins, "The Cloaking of Justice: The Supreme Court's Role in the Application of Western Law to America's Indigenous Peoples," *Wicazo Sa Review*, Spring 1994.

Index